Essential Series

 University of Hertfordshire

Learning and Information Services

Springer

London
Berlin
Heidelberg
New York
Barcelona
Hong Kong
Milan
Paris
Singapore
Tokyo

Aladdin Ayesh

Essential
Dynamic HTML
fast

**Developing an
Interactive Web Site**

Springer

Aladdin Ayesh, BSc, MSc
Department of Computer and Information Sciences,
De Montfort University, Kents Hill Campus, Hammerwood Gate,
Kents Hill, Milton Keynes MK7 6HP, UK

Series Editor
John Cowell, BSc (Hons), MPhil, PhD
Department of Computer and Information Sciences,
De Montfort University, Kents Hill Campus, Hammerwood Gate,
Kents Hill, Milton Keynes MK7 6HP, UK

ISSN 1439-975X

ISBN 1-85233-626-9 Springer-Verlag London Berlin Heidelberg

British Library Cataloguing in Publication Data
A catalogue record for this book is available from the British Library

Library of Congress Cataloging-in-Publication Data
Ayesh, Aladdin, 1972-
    Essential dynamic HTML fast : developing an interactive web site. / Aladdin Ayesh
        p. cm. – (Essential series)
    Includes bibligraphical references and index.
    ISBN 1-85233-626-9 (alk. paper)
    1. DHTML (Document markup language) I. Title. II. Essential series
        (Springer-Verlag)
    QA76.76.H94 A99 2000-04-17
    005.7'2—dc21   00-037374

Typesetting: Camera-ready by author
Printed and bound at The Cromwell Press, Trowbridge, Wiltshire
34/3830-543210 Printed on acid-free paper SPIN 10731679

Contents

1

Introduction

Introduction

The Internet and the World Wide Web (WWW) have grown enormously in the last few years. Almost every adult and child has experienced the Internet through emailing friends, viewing web pages or even shopping as the expansion of the Internet in all countries, especially in the UK and the US, exceeded all imaginations. The World Wide Web has made the Internet even more attractive by providing a user friendly interface and bringing other Internet programs such as email systems within that interface. Using a browser we can open a web page document that resides on a server which is in the same town or a different country and we can communicate with people from all over the world. Additionally e-commerce, or using the Internet for business, is making the Internet and the WWW a part of our daily life and not just a leisure activity.

One of the most surprising aspects of the WWW is that almost anyone can have a web page or a web site on the Internet. People have web pages for their pets, hobbies or more serious issues. Even children have their own web pages and find it great fun to keep in touch with their friends from all over the world using email. You can do it too. This book is designed to help you to create your own attractive web site using state of the art web authoring.

In this chapter we are going to cover the terminology of the Internet and its key aspects. What is a server? What do we mean by a browser? And so on. First of all we will examine the Client/Server model which the Internet is based upon. Then we will explore HTML including browsers and editors. This chapter is an important background for the following chapters.

Who is this book for?

This book is designed to serve a wide range of readers who want to develop professional looking web pages with DHTML. You do not need to know HTML to implement web sites using DHTML as this book starts with an introduction to HTML and then shows how to bring HTML pages to life using DHTML.

If you have experience in writing HTML web pages or using some HTML editing tools you may like to jump straight to chapter 5, which will give you a smooth introduction to the DHTML world through studying interactive sites.

If you are just interested in DHTML then you may like to start from chapter 7. If you do so you must ensure that you have mastered the basics of HTML.

Client/Server model

Internet is based on the idea of the Client/Server model of networking. The server is the physical place where the information is stored and the server software is the software that controls access to this information. However users do not see the server or its software, they only see the information through the client software. For example, the Netscape browser is a client software, and is the only medium through which the user can interact with the server. It is very likely that you will receive the client software from your Internet Service Provider (ISP).

The ISP is the company that holds the server which you will use to get through to the Internet. When you create your web site you need to put that site on your ISP server. If your ISP provides you with web space they will usually designate a directory or a virtual web server for you to host your web site.

HTML tags

HTML (Hyper Text Markup Language) is based on setting (markup) marks (tags) within the text. These marks or tags determine the presentation of the page. HTML is also hyper, in other words an HTML document does not need to be read sequentially like a book. Instead it can be accessed from any point within a set of HTML documents. We will refer to an HTML document as a web page and we will refer to a set of HTML documents as a web site. Chapter 2 covers the basic HTML tags that you need to know to create your first web page. We will be using these tags through out the rest of this book.

Hands-on HTML

The simplest way to write an HTML document is to use a simple text editor. Any text editor will be appropriate including Notepad with Windows or a DOS editor.

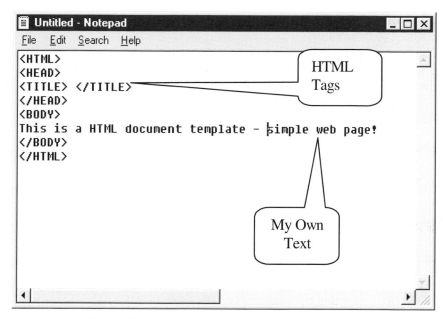

Fig1.1 *Writing an HTML document using Notepad.*

The downside of using a text editor is that you have to remember all the HTML tags you are using, as well as ensuring that the syntax is correct. The problem is tackled in this book by listing all the HTML tags after each example, thus enabling you to successfully master HTML coding. You will find it especially useful when you work with more advanced HTML tags which many HTML editors and tools do not support.

Assisting HTML editors

If you think that there are too many desk top publishing programs, you will be amazed at the number of HTML editors. There is an almost endless list of HTML editors that you can use to speed your web pages production. Six of the most popular are:

- CoffeeCup HTML Editor Express.
- HotDog Professional 5 editor.
- Hot Wax Pro editor.
- MS HTML tools.
- Netscape Composer.
- MS FrontPage.

Figure 1.2 shows the CoffeeCup HTML Editor Express which aims to be a fast way to produce a web page with links and images.

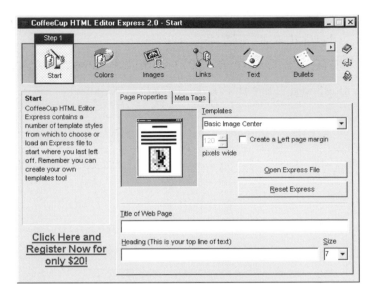

Fig 1.2 *CoffeeCup HTML Editor Express.*

The user interface of the opening form is badly designed, however it is reasonably cheap to buy and claims to direct you through the process of creating an HTML document step by step. If you are patient and prefer to spend time becoming familiar with this program's commands instead of learning HTML tags it might be just what you are looking for.

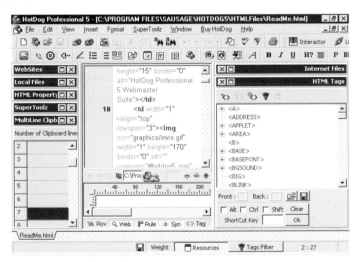

Fig1.3 *HotDog Professional 5 editor.*

The HotDog editor shown in figure 1.3 is an interesting editor with unusual sound effects. It certainly makes working with HTML fun. However, there are too many windows to work with, it is not clear whether HotDog produces frames and forms or not and a sound understanding of HTML tags is necessary.

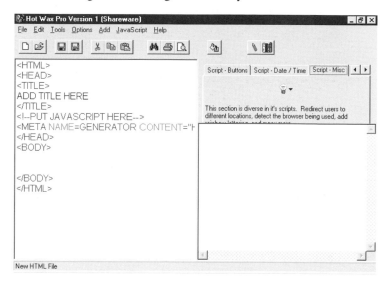

Fig 1.4 *Hot Wax Pro editor.*

The Hot Wax Pro editor shown in figure 1.4 is a more professional editor suitable for working with HTML and JavaScript. It assists you in writing HTML documents but you still have to work with HTML tags and coding directly; so again a good understanding of HTML is needed in using this editor.

These are just some samples of HTML editors which are available. Your choice of editor depends on your needs and the level of professionalism which you are aiming at. A word of warning; most of these editors have limitations. While they cover the basic HTML tags, in many cases they do not cover the more complicated HTML tags such as frames and forms. In addition, many of them do not support the new and extended HTML tags that are used in DHTML.

MS HTML tools (MS Word, MS Publisher)

Microsoft has developed HTML editing tools and attaches them to most of its products. They are easy and fast to use but have their limitations. Figure 1.5 shows how to open a new HTML document in MS Word. A template is provided and all we need to do is to select that template and write our text as we do with an ordinary Word document. To finish we save the document as an HTML document and we have a web page. This is an easy way for people who are experienced in using MS Word and are not interested in producing interactive complex sites.

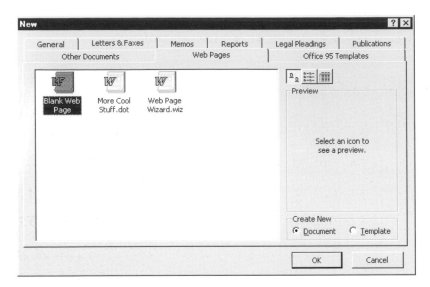

Fig 1.5 MS Word HTML templates.

Figure 1.6 shows the MS HTML editing tools in MS Publisher where more HTML templates are provided. The overall idea follows the principles applied with MS Word. If you are experienced with MS Word and MS HTML editing tools then MS Publisher is an easy way to build web pages.

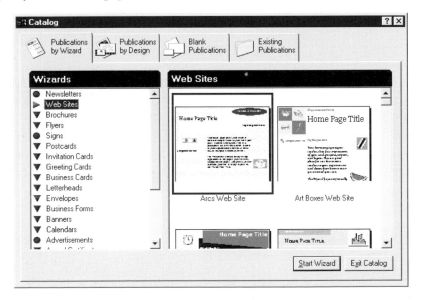

Fig 1.6 MS Publisher 98 HTML Wizard.

The limitations of MS HTML editing tools appear once we start considering complex web sites that use frames, JavaScript or DHTML technology. Although you cannot automatically generate DHTML codes with these tools, they do at least allow you to access the generated HTML tags to add further DHTML codes.

Netscape Composer

Netscape Composer comes with Netscape Communicator. It is a good tool for developing a fast but simple web site with a visual representation but it is similar to MS HTML editing tools in terms of its limitations. If you want to produce an interactive web site you may find Netscape Composer holds you back from exploring the full potential of DHTML. Figure 1.7 shows Netscape Composer after drawing a table. It does not take more than few seconds to do this and produces over ten lines of code.

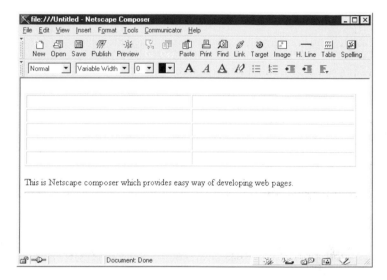

Fig 1.7 *Netscape Composer.*

If you are going to use Netscape composer or MS editing tools, identify the one you find most easy to use and know its limitations. Once you identify them you can work around them. These tools are time saving in most cases but we should not let them hold us back from exploring the powerful DHTML technology.

MS FrontPage

MS FrontPage shown in figure 1.8 is one of the most sophisticated web publishing editors. It runs with MS personal web server, which makes it a complete package to speed the production of your web page.

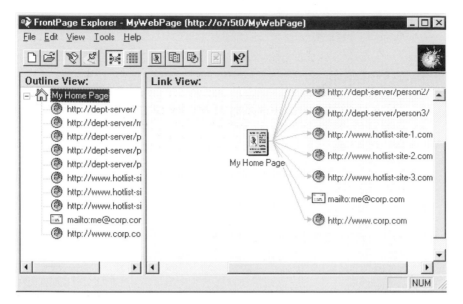

Fig 1.8 MS FrontPage.

That, however, does not mean it is without limitations. Yet again a good understanding of HTML and web authoring is needed to gain the greatest benefits from using a program like FrontPage.

Browsers

The number of web browsers is increasing rapidly. Figures 1.9, 1.10, and 1.11 show three of the most widely used browsers. Figure 1.9 shows Netscape Communicator which is the latest Netscape browser. Figure 1.10 shows the Opera browser, which is less well known but easy to use with many helpful features making it a competitive option. Figure 1.11 shows MS Internet Explorer, a well known browser. In fact MS IE and Netscape are competing strongly to dominate the market. This competition has led them to extend HTML and develop it fast as we will see in later chapters when we discuss Netscape layers and Microsoft Document Object Model (DOM).

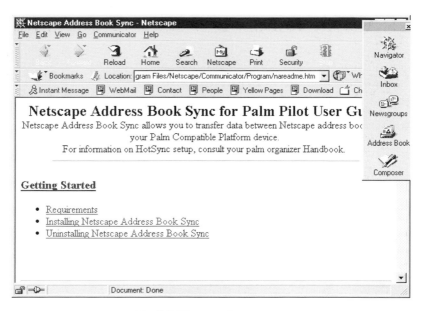

Fig 1.9 Netscape browser.

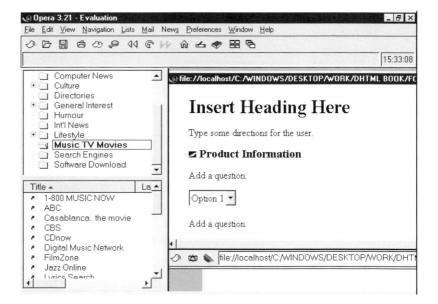

Fig 1.10 Opera browser.

Fig 1.11 Microsoft Internet Explorer browser.

Most of these browsers are distributed free. In fact you can download them over the Internet from the companies' sites. In the appendix of this book you will find the web site addresses for Netscape and Microsoft. Always try to get the latest versions as the pace of developing the Internet and extending HTML is much faster than any other technology.

What you need to use this book

All you need to use this book is an enthusiasm to learn DHTML and the following tools:

- Text editor or HTML editor that allows you to work with HTML tags directly.
- Browser; it is advisable to use either Netscape or MS Internet Explorer.
- Graphics package if available.

I will also be giving tips on how to find lots of multimedia resources over the Internet, so if you do not have a scanner or a sound package there is no need to worry.

2
Getting Started

Introduction

HTML uses tags to organise the layout and content of web pages. In this chapter we are going to look at some of the more common HTML tags as the first stage in creating our web pages. Some familiarity with common HTML tags is assumed in the rest of this book.

HTML tags determine the presentation of the page being displayed. Any HTML document is a piece of text that embodies some of these tags. Most of HTML tags are formed from two sections: an opening which is usually a letter or reserved word in < >, and a closing tag which is usually the same letter or reserved word in </>. However, you may find a few exceptions such as **<P>**. In this chapter some of the topics we will cover are:

- An HTML template.
- Font tags.
- Writing a first web page.

HTML template: blank page

Any HTML document has a standard template to which additional tags are added. This template takes the following form with the basic HTML tags:

> *<HTML>*
> *<HEAD>*

```
<TITLE>Untitled</TITLE>
</HEAD>
<BODY>
</BODY>
</HTML>
```

The first tag you see in this template is **<HTML>** ... **</HTML>** tag. This tag identifies the document to the browser as an HTML document.

The second tag is **<HEAD>** ... **</HEAD>** which identifies the header of the **HTML** document. In the header of an HTML document you may have tags that set the characteristics of the web page. One of these tags is the title tag **<TITLE>** ... **</TITLE>** which gives the page's title. This particular page is untitled. Note the 'untitled' title of the page next to the Netscape logo on the title bar in figure 2.1.

The **<BODY>** ... **</BODY>** tag marks the main body of the document (i.e. text, tags, and so on) which is shown by the browser.

Fig 2.1 My first web page.

General HTML tags

As we have seen, while most HTML tags have a closing tag, there are some exceptions. For example:

- **<P>** tag starts a new line. Pressing the *Return* or *Enter* key on the keyboard is not enough in an HTML document to start a new line even though it is the way to do so in most word processors and text editors.
- **
** tag forces the text to end regardless of the size of the browser. In other words if you maximise your browser the lines do not change, as would be the case if **
** tag was not used.
- **<HR>** tag draws a breaking line. This tag helps in dividing the page into sections.

Font tags

It is straightforward in HTML to control not only the content of your web pages, but also the font, which is used in presenting that content. HTML has a set of tags that allow you to format your text into different font styles. These tags are:

- Font size: **<FONT SIZE=1>** ... **</FONT>**
- Underline: **<U>** ... **</U>**
- Italic: **<I>** ... **</I>**
- Bold: **<B>** ... **</B>**

An example of using these tags is shown in figure 2.2.

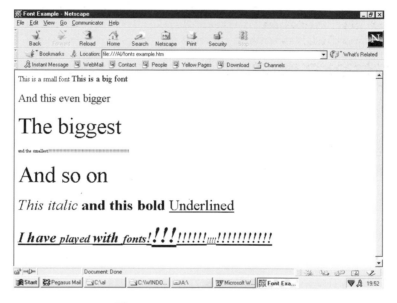

Fig 2.2 *Using different fonts.*

The HTML code that I have used to produce these different fonts is:

*This is a small font<**FONT SIZE=4**>This is a big font<**/FONT**>*
*<**P**>*
*<**FONT SIZE=5**>And this even bigger<**/FONT**>*
*<**P**>*
*<**FONT SIZE=7**>The biggest<**/FONT**>*
*<**P**>*
*<**FONT SIZE=1**>*
and the smallest!!
*<**/FONT**>*
*<**P**>*
*<**FONT SIZE=7**>And so on<**BR**>*
*<**/FONT**>*

```
<P>
<I><FONT SIZE=6>This italic </FONT></I>
<B><FONT SIZE=6>and this bold </FONT></B>
<U><FONT SIZE=6>Underlined</FONT></U>
<P>
<U><I><B><FONT SIZE=6>I have</FONT>
<FONT SIZE=5>played</FONT>
<FONT SIZE=6>with</FONT><FONT SIZE=5>fonts</FONT>
<FONT SIZE=6>!</FONT><FONT SIZE=7>!!!</FONT>
<FONT SIZE=6>!!!!!!</FONT>!!!!
<FONT SIZE=6>!!!!!!!!!!!!</FONT></B></I></U>
```

Notice the nested tags. You could use many different tags within each other to manipulate your text and derive various effects. You may like to have some fun exploring these effects which would give your web pages a personal touch.

Using headers

Headers provide pre-formatted text styles. There are six different header styles; here are some of them. The tag that is used is **H** from header and the number of the header style (i.e. 1, 2, …, 6).

```
<H1>This is header one</H1>
<H2>This is header two</H2>
...
...
<H6>and I am header six ahhhhhhhhhhhhhhhhhh how small!</H6>
```

I have used this code to create figure 2.3.

Fig 2.3 *Using headers.*

Alignment tags

There are two alignment tags available in HTML, **LEFT** and **CENTER**. The default is **LEFT**. In figure 2.4 the default is shown by the sentence:

> *I am at the left.*

To centre your text you need to use **CENTER** tag as I have done with the centred text in figure 2.4, and apply the following line of code:

> *<CENTER>I am in the centre. </CENTER>*

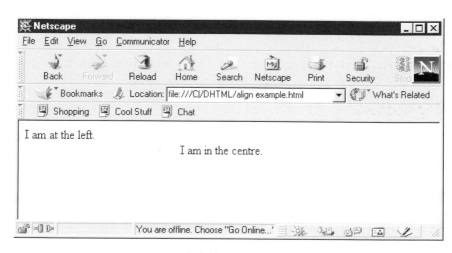

Figure 2.4 Alignment of text.

First web page

Now we are ready to start our first web page. You may like to have an introductory page about yourself and your reasons for being on the net. I am going to construct my own first web page, which contains basic information about me and how I feel about being on the Internet for the first time.

The first step is to construct the template of the web page with a head and a body. I am going to give the page the title *First web page example-simple* using the tag **TITLE**. The result is an empty page as in figure 2.1.

The second step is to divide the web page into sections and write the headers of these sections. *Aladdin's on the Internet* forms the header of the page. Let us divide the text body into sections as shown in figure 2.5, where *My magical lamp* is to attract attention while *What this is about!* is an introductory part about the aim of this web page.

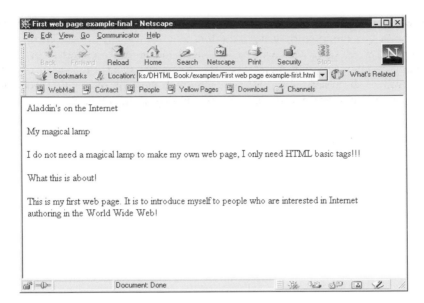

Fig. 2.5 *A simple first web page.*

Once the material is in place we can change the fonts and the presentation of the material to make it more attractive. Figure 2.6 shows the same web page after I have used a few more font tags.

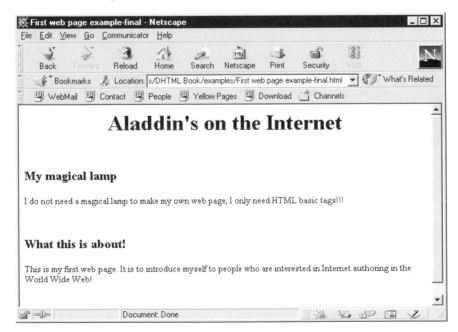

Fig 2.6 *A more organised first web page using headers and font tags.*

The web page in figure 2.6 is more clearly presented and so more eye-catching, and could be further modified by using more font tags. However, the detrimental effect of overusing font or other tags will be illustrated in the next chapters. In chapters 4 (Frames), 5 (Interactive Sites) and 9 (Background and Layout) the aspects of web page design will be discussed. Once we are happy with the look of our first web page, we save it into a file to use it again later on the building of the whole site. Let us call this file *page1.html*.

3
Organising Your Data

Introduction

When you are creating a web page it is important to be clear about the information you want to put on the page and how you want to display it. This is examined in further detail in chapter 9, but for the moment we will look at some HTML tags that enable us to organise the data and to represent it in a more readable format.

We also need to consider how relevant this data is to the current web page and if we should have more than one web page. In this chapter we are going to continue to construct our own personal web site, and some of the topics covered will help us to organise our data and construct our first web site. They are:

- Lists.
- Tables.
- Links and hypertext.

Lists

Lists are a convenient way of presenting items in numerical order or unordered. While you may like to do this by hand, HTML allows you to do it through assigned tags. You may like to start a new web page (similar to the template we saw in the previous chapter) and think of things you would like to list on your own personal or professional web page.

Unordered lists

You may have a list of items where the order is not important. If you feel there is no need to emphasise any of these items, the list is unordered. The unordered list tag is <UL> ... </UL>.

In this block, each list item needs to be prefaced with the tag <LI> which indicates the following is a list item. Figure 3.1 shows the completed page.

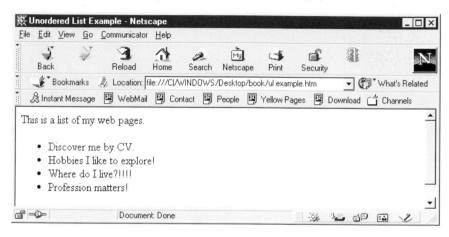

Fig 3.1 Unordered list of my web pages.

The HTML code that produces this page is:

> *This is a list of my web pages.*
> *<UL>*
> *<LI>Discover me by CV.*
> *<LI>Hobbies I like to explore!*
> *<LI>Where do I live?!!!!*
> *<LI>Profession matters!
*
> *
*
> *
*
> *</UL>*

Ordered lists

When some items in a list are more important that others you can use an ordered list. By using the ordered list tags the items will be given the appropriate numbers in the list. Figure 3.2 shows the list of qualities that I should like my ideal date to possess in order of importance. This may become part of my personal introduction page. You may like to make an ordered list of hobbies, goals in life or an action list. The ordered list tag is <OL> ... </OL>. The list item tag is still in use to identify the list items.

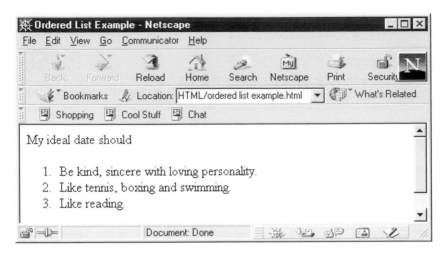

Fig 3.2 *Ordered list of my ideal date.*

The HTML code that is used to produce the above page is:

> *My ideal date should*
> *<OL>*
> *<LI>Be kind, sincere with loving personality.*
> *<LI>Like tennis, boxing and swimming.*
> *<LI>Like reading.
*
> *
*
> *
*
> *</OL>*

Creating tables

A table is a very common form of representing data. It gives you a way to represent relationships between different categories, for example between people and the tasks they have to do. To present your data in a table format you need to use:

- <TABLE> ... </TABLE> tag to create a table.
- <TR> ... </TR> tag to add a row in the table.
- <TD> ... </TD> tag to control individual cells.

Figure 3.3 shows a timetable of a tennis league at work. You can build your own table which might be a timetable of a game you play with friends, tasks for your employees, a booking table, and so on.

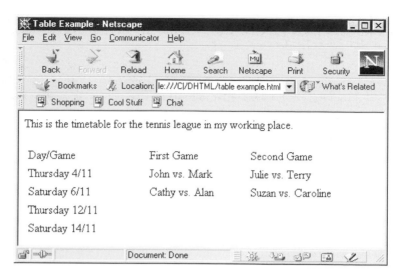

***Fig 3.3** Timetable for a tennis league.*

The HTML code that produces figure 3.3:

*This is the timetable for the tennis league in my working place.
*
<P>
<TABLE>
<TR>
<TD WIDTH=197>Day/Game</TD>
<TD WIDTH=197>First Game</TD>
<TD WIDTH=197>Second Game</TD>
</TR>
<TR>
<TD WIDTH=197>Thursday 4/11</TD>
<TD WIDTH=197>John vs. Mark</TD>
<TD WIDTH=197>Julie vs. Terry</TD>
</TR>
<TR>
<TD WIDTH=197>Saturday 6/11</TD>
<TD WIDTH=197>Cathy vs. Alan</TD>
<TD WIDTH=197>Suzan vs. Caroline</TD>
</TR>
<TR>
<TD WIDTH=197>Thursday 12/11</TD>
<TD WIDTH=197></TD>
<TD WIDTH=197></TD>
</TR>
<TR>
<TD WIDTH=197>Saturday 14/11</TD>
<TD WIDTH=197></TD>

```
<TD WIDTH=197></TD>
</TR>
</TABLE>
```

Let us take the following extract:

```
<TR>
<TD WIDTH=197>Day/Game</TD>
<TD WIDTH=197>First Game</TD>
<TD WIDTH=197>Second Game</TD>
</TR>
```

We are going to look at this in order to understand the tags that are used within the structured table tag. This example represents a row in the table. It starts with the row tag **<TR>** followed by the data tag **<TD>** which identifies the cells within that row. Each cell in the row is represented by a data tag. There are three cells which, when put together with the other rows that have three cells in them, form three columns. The **WIDTH** attribute represents the width of the cell. It is important to keep the right width between the relevant cells in the different rows to produce a neat table. The contents of each cell comes between **<TD>** and its closing tag **</TD>**.

Links and hypertext

It is a good idea to practice dividing the information you are presenting into sections, pages or any other module formats you like. To link these together you need to use the link tag **<A>**. Links can be external or internal.

External links connect our web page to other people's web pages, while internal links hold our own web pages together. Figure 3.4 shows my bookmark web page that contains links to external sites.

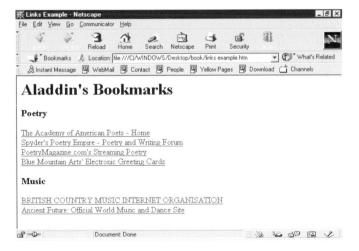

Fig. 3.4 *My bookmarks page with links to external sites.*

The HTML code of the links that are presented in the above page is:

> *<H3>Poetry</H3>*
> *<A HREF="http://www.poets.org/" >The Academy of American Poets - Home</A>*
> *<P>*
> *<A HREF="http://www.spydersempire.com/poetry.htm" >Spyder's Poetry Empire - Poetry and Writing Forum</A>*
> *<P>*
> *<A HREF="http://www.poetrymagazine.com/real/index.htm" > PoetryMagazine.com's Streaming Poetry</A>*
> *<P>*
> *<A HREF="http://www.bluemountain.com/index.html">Blue Mountain Arts' Electronic Greeting Cards</A>*
> *<H3>Music</H3>*
> *<A HREF="http://www.countrymusic.org.uk/index.html">BRITISH COUNTRY MUSIC INTERNET ORGANISATION</A>*
> *<P>*
> *<A HREF="http://www.ancient-future.com/">Ancient Future: Official World Music and Dance Site</A>*

Let us take the following extract as an example to study:

> *<A HREF="http://www.spydersempire.com/poetry.htm" > Spyder's Poetry Empire - Poetry and Writing Forum</A>*

First, notice how <A> tag, used as the address identified by the attribute **HREF**, is presented in quotation marks "". This address should be the full URL address if the link is external. URL address is the Internet address which one types to view a page (e.g. www.cool-linkz.com). However, if using the <A> tag to link our web pages together, then we need to use relative addressing. Relative addressing means that the web page address in the link is relative to the web page that contains the link. It enables us to move our web pages from one directory (e.g. home computer) to another (e.g. ISP server) without the need to change the addressing in the links between our web pages. As an example of relative addressing let us look at the following link:

> *<A HREF="Hobbies.htm">Hobbies</A>*

Because only the web page name is used, the browser will look in the same directory for that file. This will prove very useful as we move further towards building a full site which usually contains many web pages linked to each other.

Notice that we usually add a descriptive text (*Spyder's Poetry Empire - Poetry and Writing Forum* in this example) before closing the tag with </A>. When browsed, the text that is used to title the link will usually appear on the screen in underlined blue to indicate that is a link. The colour may vary depending on the settings on your computer. It is important to use meaningful titles for the links as that is what may or may not attract the viewer to follow that link.

The internal links will be used in the next section when we build our first web site, using the web pages we constructed in the previous chapter and sections of this chapter.

We can also use **<A>** tag to provide links for email. You may have noticed on most web pages that there seems to be a link with text such as *email me here* or *you can contact me at* and so on (see figure 3.5). And when you click on that link you find the email window is opened and the email address appears in the *To* field of the message (see figure 3.6).

Fig 3.5 *Using <A> tag to insert an email link.*

Fig 3.6 *An email window opens when we click on the email link.*

Here is the code you need to enable your page viewers to email you over the web:

```
<HTML>
<HEAD>
<TITLE>Aayesh</TITLE>
</HEAD>
<BODY>
<B><FONT FACE=Arial SIZE=4><P>Contact</P>
</B></FONT><P>You can contact me via email @ the following
address:</P>
<P>
<A HREF="mailto:Aayesh@dmu.ac.uk">aayesh@dmu.ac.uk</A>
</P>
</BODY>
</HTML>
```

First web site

Now you can start building your first web site using the HTML tags presented so far.
You may use font tags to make your web pages more interesting, lists and tables to
present your data and links to bind the whole site together. The web pages we have
created so far consist of an index page, hobbies and ideal date page, tennis league page
and an optional introductory page. You may like to create your own pages, for example
a CV page. I have created an index file that brings together some of the web pages we
saw earlier in this chapter. An index.html page is usually the first page that runs on a
site.

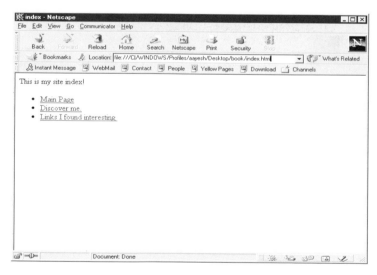

Fig 3.7 *Index page with links to the other web pages in my site.*

Here is the code you need to write your own index page:

```
<HTML>
<HEAD>
<TITLE>index</TITLE>
</HEAD>
<BODY>
<P>This is my site index!</P>
<UL>
<LI><A HREF="Main.html">Main Page</A></LI>
<LI><A HREF="DiscoverMe.html">Discover me.</A></LI>
<LI><A HREF="MyLinks.html">Links I found interesting </A></LI>
</UL>
</BODY>
</HTML>
```

4
Frames

Introduction

In this chapter you will be introduced to the wonderful world of frames. Frames allow you to tie your web pages together in style, giving the viewer an interesting presentation and an easy way to navigate your site.

Unfortunately many web page editors (e.g. Netscape Composer) do not have the tools to build frames and so we need, in most cases, to write the HTML code directly. There is a set of four new tags which we have to apply to add frames to our application:

- The **FRAMESET** tag.
- The **FRAME** tag.
- The **TARGET** attribute.
- The **NOFRAME** tag.

What are frames?

Before we look at the HTML tags, we need to understand what you can use frames for. Frames are an extended feature of HTML that allows you to divide the screen into windows. The advantage being that you can view more than one web page at a time.

As an example, let us refer back to the web pages we produced in the last chapter. It would be helpful if we could keep the index page in view while we navigate through the other pages, and to do so we need to use a frame. The index is usually kept resident in one frame, while the contents of the pages being navigated through, is viewed in another frame. Figure 4.1 shows the use of frames in the *Hemmington Scott Ltd* site.

Fig 4.1 *An existing web site that uses frames.*

To use frames we need to do two things:

- Create a file containing the frame setting.
- Modify the index page so that the links *target* the frame which is used for viewing.

To do this, there are two HTML tags, **FRAMESET** and **FRAME**.

FRAMESET tag

The **FRAMESET** tag defines the start and the end of the set of frames. The basic format of the **FRAMESET** tag is:

<FRAMESET COLS="20%, 80%">

The **COLS** attribute refers to columns. In other words the frames will divide the screen into columns. The percentage that appears afterwards defines two things. First, the number of parameters shown indicates the number of frames that are used. In this case there are two frames. Second the value of percentage states the space each corresponding frame will take from the screen. Figure 4.2 shows an example of column based frames.

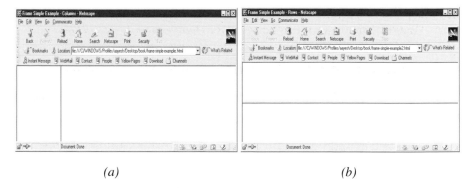

(a)   (b)

Fig 4.2 *Simple frames.*

The code that is used to produce figure 4.2 (a) is:

```
<FRAMESET COLS="20%, 80%">
<FRAME>
<FRAME>
</FRAMESET>
```

The code that is used to produce the page shown in figure 4.2 (b) is:

```
<FRAMESET ROWS="50%, 50%">
<FRAME>
<FRAME>
</FRAMESET>
```

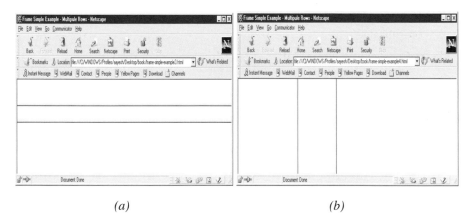

(a)   (b)

Fig 4.3 *Multiple frames in one* **FRAMESET**.

The code that is used to produce figure 4.3 (a) is:

```
<FRAMESET ROWS="30%, 20%,60%">
<FRAME>
```

```
<FRAME>
<FRAME>
</FRAMESET>
```

The code that is used to produce the page shown in figure 4.3 (b) is:

```
<FRAMESET COLS="30%, 20%,60%">
<FRAME>
<FRAME>
<FRAME>
</FRAMESET>
```

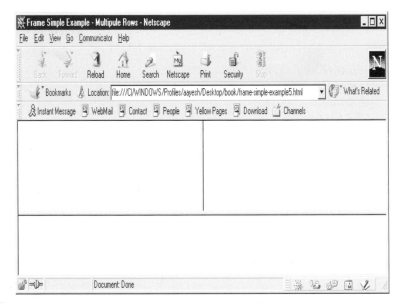

Fig 4.4 *Multiple frames in multiple **FRAMESETS**.*

The code that is used to produce the multiple frames shown in figure 4.4 is:

```
<FRAMESET ROWS="30%, 20%">
<FRAMESET COLS="50%, 50%">
<FRAME>
<FRAME>
</FRAMESET>
<FRAME>
</FRAMESET>
```

Notice that in all the previous examples, the **COLS** attribute represents the number of columns while the **ROWS** attribute presents the number of rows. Also note that the percentages that we give to these rows or columns have to add up to 100 per cent. You can have as many frame sets embedded in each other as you wish.

Storyboarding

As we have seen in the previous section, frames can be designed in complicated patterns. Storyboarding is an easy technique which can simplify the designing of your web site. You basically draw boxes which represent the different screens, and in each box roughly draw how you would like the screen to look. The next step is to find the means to implement it through different combinations of **FRAMESET** and **FRAME** tags. The storyboarding technique will be explored again in chapter 9.

FRAME tag

Once you have made the settings for your frames, the **FRAME** tag provides a handle to each frame that is represented in the frame set. Let us take the first frame set example:

```
<FRAMESET COLS="20%, 80%">
<FRAME>
<FRAME>
</FRAMESET>
```

It is telling us there are two frames in this set. This is a typical frame setting where the left frame is used to show the index of the site and the right frame is used to show the contents of any chosen link from that index.

In the above example we have two **FRAME** tags that are empty. As a start let us name them using **NAME** attribute:

```
<FRAMESET COLS="20%, 80%">
<FRAME NAME=Index >
<FRAME NAME=Main>
</FRAMESET>
```

Notice that in naming a frame we try to use a conventional name that means something and is easy to remember. Obviously we will have an index in the index frame so let us add that using the source attribute.

```
<FRAME NAME =Index SRC =index.html>
```

TARGET attribute

The **TARGET** attribute is an attribute that is used with the hyperlink tag <A>. Its function is to direct the opening of the link in the targeted frame. This is why naming frames is important because we will need to use these names to refer to the different frames. If we do not use the **TARGET** attribute, the link we are opening will be opened in the same frame. In effect it will look as if we are using part of the screen for our site activities and wasting the other part. What we usually like to do is to keep the index part of our site, which contains links to our different web pages within the site, static and use the other frame to show the contents of the requested web page. To do so we need to add the **TARGET** attribute to each link in our index and we have to assign the value of this attribute to the name of the frame we want the link to open in. It is important that you use the frame name and not the file name where the frame set is and that you give each frame a different name, different to the file name that contains it. We will see how to use the **TARGET** attribute in a practical example using frames, but first we must look at the **NOFRAME** tag.

NOFRAME tag and old browsers

Frames are an extended feature of HTML. Not all browsers support frames especially old versions of Mosaic and Netscape. This means if your web site uses frames, it will not be viewable on some browsers.

There are two ways to handle this: the first way is to create an entry web page that allows the user to choose between two versions one with frames and another without. This way will double the work.

The alternative is to use the **NOFRAME** tag after or before the **FRAMESET** tag. To my surprise, I could not find a recent version of any of the main browsers that does not support frames. However here is the code that you need to add to your frames file to handle frame challenged browsers:

> *<NOFRAME>*
> *This browser does not support frames.*
> *… or any other message and maybe a link to an alternative non-frame*
> *version of your site.*
> *</NOFRAME>*
> *<FRAMESET>*
> *… your frames come in here …*
> *</FRAMESET>*

First web site

It is exciting putting together your first web site. We do not need to write new web pages, we can use the pages we have created in previous chapters make a web site through linking the web pages using frames. Here are the results using the pages I have created:

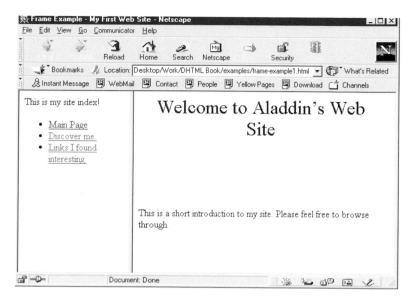

Fig 4.5 *The main page.*

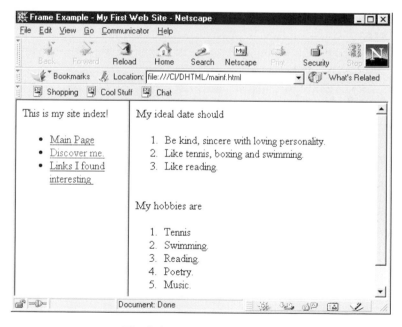

Fig 4.6 *Discover me page.*

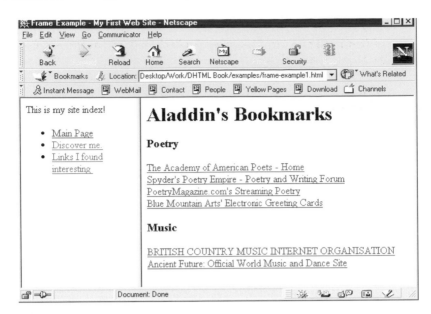

Fig 4.7 *Links web page.*

The code I used in the base file that contains the **FRAMESET** tag, is the file that you should open first:

```
<HTML>
<HEAD>
<TITLE>Frame Example - My First Web Site</TITLE>
</HEAD>
<FRAMESET COLS="30%, 70%">
<FRAME NAME="index" SRC="index.html">
<FRAME NAME="main" SRC="main.html">
</FRAMESET>
</HTML>
```

Note that we did not use the **BODY** tag with frames even though a **BODY** tag forms a part of the HTML document template that we saw in chapter 2. If you do try using a **BODY** tag it is likely the code will not work. This is one of the differences between a standard HTML document and the **FRAMESET** document.

```
<HTML>
<HEAD>
<TITLE>index</TITLE>
</HEAD>
<BODY>
<P>This is my site index!</P>
<UL>
<LI><A HREF="Main.html" TARGET="main">Main Page</A></LI>
<LI><A HREF="DiscoverMe.html" TARGET="main">Discover me.</A>
```

```
</LI>
<LI><A HREF="MyLinks.html" TARGET="main">Links I found
interesting</A></LI>
</UL>
</BODY>
</HTML>
```

5
Interactive Sites

Introduction

There is no point in developing your own web pages if people do not find them attractive and interesting. An interactive site helps us to attract more viewers than a static site. In this chapter we are going to look at the features of interactive web sites with examples from existing web sites whose addresses are given in the appendix.

What does interactive mean?

An interactive site is a site that can interact and respond to the viewer. The simplest interaction, which we have experienced so far, is the hyperlinks that respond to and allow the viewer to move from one web page to another.

Why interactive?

Reasons for building interactive sites vary depending on the purpose of the site. It could be an advertising site, or personal site, or commercial site. Whatever the type of the site we are building, the use of interactive components would serve one or more of the following:

- Exchanging data.
- Displaying informative messages in response to viewers' actions.
- Displaying general informative messages and illustrations to direct viewers.
- Attracting attention.

- Creating user-friendly interfaces.

Exchanging data is very important in commercial sites. The viewer of such sites may like to exchange data with the owner of the site for many reasons, from requesting further information about a product to actually ordering a product. Automating this process allows the interaction between the viewer and the web site as if the viewer were interacting directly with the owner of the site.

Responsive action messages is an important aspect of giving the user confidence in what he or she is doing during viewing the site. These messages could vary from a welcoming message to a confirmation message or even an email with requested information; the list is endless.

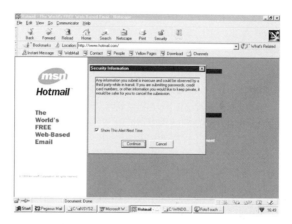

Fig 5.1 *A responsive message of login action to Hotmail.*

Informative messages and illustrations (images, graphics, and so on) usually guide the viewer through the web site. They are vital in attracting viewers and making the navigation through the site easy and pleasant. People and companies are on the web to present themselves to the outside world. This aspect of interaction is the most important consideration when building any web site.

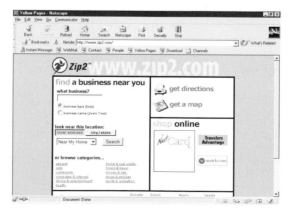

Fig 5.2 *Informative images and animations in Yellow Pages.*

The following section presents some of the ways of making a site interactive. Using one or more of these techniques depends on which aspects we want to serve within the site we are building.

Ways to build an interactive site

There are many ways to make a site interactive. When we decide on the design of a site we need to consider the requirements of the targeted viewers. In other words why do we want our site to be interactive? Do we want to keep a guest book on our personal web site or to allow the user to request information and receive that information by email? Is it for commercial or personal use? The reasons are endless and we should identify our requirement before we make our site interactive.

We can make our site interactive in a variety of ways:

- Forms are a means of getting information from the viewer. This information could be comments, registration or enquiry, product order and so on.
- Messages are a means of responding to the viewer. This could be by text appearing directly on the screen or by an email message. Messages have many roles such as a warning, confirmation, and so on.
- Change in content is one of the main features that differentiates DHTML from HTML. It provides us with the flexibility of changing the view (for example, the text) that is represented to the viewer. This change (be it in colour, format of presentation or complete change of content) can be used to create a more attractive and informative site.
- Change in images provides similar effects to change in content. Additionally it may provide extra details of the image (such as an icon image becoming full sized).
- Sound provides an alternative responding tool as well as attraction. Background sound may establish the mood of the site, as discussed in chapter 8.
- Change in positioning is another feature of DHTML that does not exist in HTML. It provides attraction and energises the site by changing the positioning of text, images and so on.

Note that change in content and positioning are extensions made to HTML. HTML and dynamic changes in content and positioning are known as Dynamic HTML (DHTML). DHTML also includes scripting such as JavaScript.

6

Forms

Introduction

Exchanging data with the viewer of our web site is important. This data could be a viewer's comments, an information request, a product order and so on. Figure 6.1 shows a subscription form where viewers can send their details for subscription over the Internet.

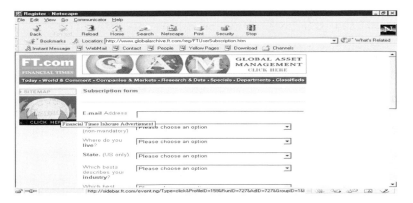

Fig 6.1 *Subscription form of the Financial Times.*

Forms also provide a front end (i.e. a user interface) for databases to be accessed over the Internet. That enables users to search the database or add records to it. Figure

6.2 shows a form used to search a database of advertisements on the Classifieds2000 web site.

Fig 6.2 Searching Classifieds2000 database ads of convertible cars.

In this chapter you will learn how to create and use forms using HTML. Some of the topics we will cover are:

- The **FORM** tag.
- The **METHOD** and **ACTION** attribute.
- The **SELECT** tag.
- The **INPUT** tag.

FORM tag

The **FORM** tag is a structured tag, which means it provides a capsule which other tags are gathered within. The simplest format of the **FORM** tag is:

> *<FORM>*
> *</FORM>*

Figure 6.3 shows a simple example of a form where some components are added such as options boxes, text boxes and command buttons.

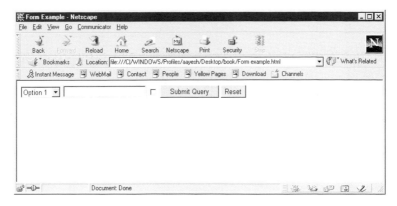

Fig 6.3 *Simple form.*

The code that is used to implement this form is:

```
<FORM>
<SELECT>
<OPTION VALUE="Option 1">Option 1
<OPTION VALUE="Option 2">Option 2
<OPTION VALUE="Option 3">Option 3
</SELECT>
<INPUT TYPE="TEXT" MAXLENGTH="50" NAME="First name">
<INPUT TYPE="CHECKBOX">
<INPUT TYPE="SUBMIT">
<INPUT TYPE="RESET">
</FORM>
```

As each of the tags within this example may take more than one attribute and may include more tags, it is better to discuss each tag separately in more detail.

SELECT tag and OPTION tag

The task of the **SELECT** tag is to provide the user with a list of exclusive options to choose from. It forces the exclusive relationship between the options so that the user can only choose one option. These options are encapsulated within the **SELECT** tag:

```
<SELECT>
</SELECT>
```

We present these options within the **SELECT** tag using another tag that we call the **OPTION** tag. For each set of options we want to present to the user we have to have an option tag in front of it, as we can see in this excerpt from the previous example:

```
<OPTION VALUE ="Option 1">Option 1
```

The **VALUE** attribute assigns a value to the option so we can use it in a conditional statement during data manipulation. This will be useful information when we reach chapter 17 on scripting and JavaScript.

INPUT tag

The **INPUT** tag allows us to receive the user input which can be in various formats as shown in figure 6.3. Each format maps to a HTML tag, which we use to indicate which format we want the user input to take. Here is an extract from the example:

```
<INPUT TYPE="TEXT" MAXLENGTH="50" NAME ="First name">
<INPUT TYPE="CHECKBOX">
<INPUT TYPE="SUBMIT">
<INPUT TYPE="RESET">
```

As we can see, the **INPUT** tag has a **TYPE** attribute which defines the format of the user's input. Depending on the input format, we may add extra attributes.

METHOD and ACTION attributes of FORM tag

If you re-write the above code to implement the form presented in figure 6.3, and then press submit nothing will happen! The reason is that the **FORM** tag has not been told what to do when an action is taken. To tell the **FORM** tag what to do with the information submitted we use two attributes: **METHOD** and **ACTION**.

The **METHOD** attribute is the most straightforward. It always has one of two values: **POST** and **GET**. The difference between the two methods is the way data is transformed. We use the **GET** method when we want the server to request data. It usually imposes more restrictions on how the data is received, but it is unlikely that you will need to use this method at this stage. The **POST** method is more commonly used, and is applied to post our forms after the user has filled them in. In order for us to post our forms we have to tell the **FORM** tag what action it has to take and we do this by using the **ACTION** attribute. The **ACTION** attribute will usually have one of two values, either the URL address of a program on the server that is written in accordance to CGI script guidelines, or **mailto**. The code you need to add to your **FORM** tag to allow the submission of information to come to your email box is as follows:

```
<FORM METHOD="POST" ACTION="mailto:Aayesh@dmu.ac.uk">
</FORM>
```

Do not forget that you have to use your email address after **mailto** instead of my email address, otherwise I will have a very busy email system!

CGI scripting

So far we have used **mailto** action to email the forms. However the received email will be unformatted information. To format the received data you need a server side program; this type of program is usually referred to as CGI scripting.

The Common Gate Interface (CGI) specifies the set of rules that have to be complied with when writing a program to manipulate information over the Internet. CGI scripting can be done in almost any language and even though it is usually used as an interface between web forms and databases, CGI script could be used to control the web pages from the server side. CGI scripting is discussed further in chapter 17.

7

Colour and Images

Introduction

Two issues that need to be considered during the design of a web page are colour and images. As mentioned in chapter 5, colour and images play an important role in interactive sites and can be used to add interest and information to the web page. Later we shall see how we can change colour and re-position images but in this chapter we shall discuss the use of colour and images in designing web pages. We shall explore the tags that are used in setting colour as well as the tags that are used to insert images within the web page. The different usage of colour and images are highlighted as it is appropriate within the relevant tags. We are going to look at:

- Font colours.
- The **IMG** tag.
- Using images as hyperlinks.
- Map images.

The chapter concludes with two main practical examples of using images as hyperlinks. The first example simulates a menu bar and the second uses client-side map images.

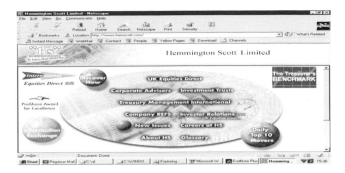

Fig 7.1 *Use of informative images on a web page.*

You can control both the background and font colours your in web page and images can be either used as background or included within the web page (front end). Figure 7.1 shows a map image where each section of the image is a hyperlink. A map image is another way of using images effectively.

Background colours

HTML provides the facility to colour the background of the web page as well as the text presented on that background. The **BGCOLOR** attribute in the **BODY** tag determines the background colour. We can use either numbers or a colour name to present the colour to the **BODY** tag. The use of numbers is dictated by the RGB colour model. RGB stands for red, green and blue, whose mixture produces the colour we see on the screen. Each colour is presented by two hexadecimal digits ranging between 0-9 and a-f. Figure 7.2 shows an example in which I used hexadecimal digits.

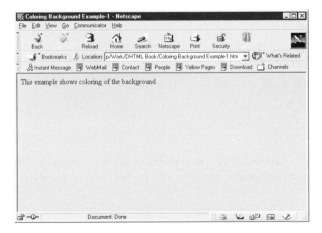

Fig 7.2 *Changing background colour.*

The code you need to change your background colour is:

```
<BODY TEXT="#000000" BGCOLOR="#00ffff">
<P>This example shows coloring of the background</P>
</BODY>
```

Notice that the **TEXT** attribute changes the colour of the text, while the **BGCOLOR** attribute changes the colour of the background. In this example I have used numbers in referring to the colours, but you could use colour names instead. Try changing the **BGCOLOR** value to *blue* and see what happens.

Font colours

Font colours can be set using the **BODY** tag or **FONT** tag. The difference between the **BODY** tag and **FONT** tag is that the attributes of the **BODY** tag set the colour value for the text in the entire document. The **FONT** tag affects only the text that is included within the tag scope.

There are many different attributes that can be used with the **BODY** tag to set colours. As we have seen, **BGCOLOR** is used to set the background colour, and the **TEXT** attribute sets the text colour within a document excluding the hyperlinks.

For hyperlinks there are three attributes that allow us to change the hyperlink colour:

- The **LINK** attribute sets the colour of the hyperlink.
- The **ALINK** attribute sets the colour of an active hyperlink.
- The **VLINK** attribute sets the colour of a visited hyperlink.

The values set using the **FONT** tag will override the values set using the **BODY** tag attributes. Here is an example using these attributes.

Fig 7.3 *Changing font and links colours.*

You will not notice the difference in colour between the Yahoo and Amazon links in figure 7.3, but you should be able to notice the different shades. Here is the code that I used to produce two different colours for my links and text.

```
<HTML>
<HEAD>
<TITLE>Links Colouring</TITLE>
</HEAD>
<BODY TEXT="black" LINK="red" VLINK="#800000"
BGCOLOR="white">
<FONT COLOR = "BLUE">
 <H1>Links Colouring </H1>
</FONT>
<P>
Here are some interesting links with different colouring.  I have used both
colour names and colour numbers in this example.
<P>
<A HREF="http://www.yahoo.com/">
<FONT COLOR="#008000">http://www.yahoo.com/</FONT>
</A>
<P>
<A HREF="http://www.amazon.com/">http://www.amazon.com/</A>
</BODY>
</HTML>
```

Images

Images in web sites can be used in a wide variety of ways. Images can be used as background, a representation tool of a navigation map or just included as part of the document contents. They may be photos, graphics, graphical patterns and so on. As there are different image types, there are different image formats such as GIF, JPEG, BMP and TIF.

The image format is a reference to the way an image is stored in a file. GIF and JPEG formats are almost all supported by graphical browsers and it is therefore sensible to try to use and save image files in these formats when we implement web pages with images. Here are some examples of existing sites that are using images.

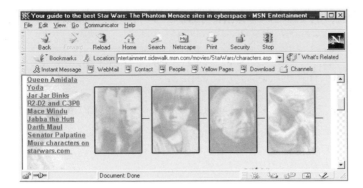

Fig 7.4 *Example of using images in the Star Wars web site.*

Fig 7.5 *Using graphical images in an e-cards site.*

Adding images to web sites is the most popular feature of most web sites. Images provide both information and appeal.

Background images

Images can be used as a background by using the **BACKGROUND** attribute in the **BODY** tag. This image could be a scanned photograph, a graphic or a graphical pattern. Here is an example of using a graphical pattern as a background.

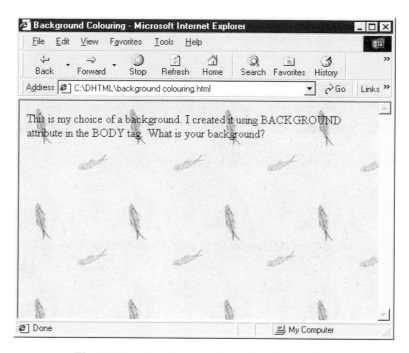

Fig 7.6 Graphical pattern-based background.

The code that I used to make my GIF file into a background on this web page is:

<BODY TEXT="#000000" BACKGROUND="background.gif">
<P>This is my choice of a background. I created it using BACKGROUND
attribute in the BODY tag. What is your background?</P>
</BODY>

Notice that the background can be any image file, but for compatibility with most browsers it should be in GIF or JEPG formats. You may use a scanned photograph, graphics, patterns and so on. You may even like to compose your own background using an image editor or graphics package, for example Microsoft Photo Editor that comes with Windows.

IMG tag

The **IMG** tag allows the insertion of an image within a document. While we can have only one background image, many different images can be included within a document. The **IMG** tag enhances various attributes. Let us start with the simple use of the **IMG** tag.

Fig 7.7 *Inserting an image within a web page using the **IMG** tag.*

This picture is included in the web page using the following code:

```
<P ALIGN="center">
<IMG SRC="images/beach4.gif"
ALT="misbeach.gif (38159 bytes)"
WIDTH="390" HEIGHT="185">
</P>
```

We may like to use some text to describe the image, which could be for example a family picture or interesting local scenery. To do so we use **ALT** attribute which demonstrates a message when the mouse moves over the picture.

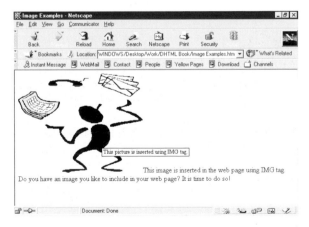

Fig 7.8 *Inserting a graphical image using the **IMG** tag.*

The code I used to add this graphic to the web page is:

*<BODY TEXT="#000000" LINK="#0000ff" VLINK="#800080"
BACKGROUND="background.gif">
<P><IMG SRC="Image4.gif" WIDTH=280 HEIGHT=220 ALT="This
picture is inserted using IMG tag.">This image is inserted in the web page
using IMG tag. Do you have an image you like to include in your web page?
It is time to do so!</P>
</BODY>*

Notice how I used the **ALT** attribute to add the message that appears when the mouse passes over the image. You can use the **ALT** attribute to add that extra professional touch by giving the viewer messages about your images, especially if you are using these images as links. We will now look at how we can use images as links.

Image link

Images can be used to present a link by using the **IMG** tag within the link tag **<A>...</A>**.

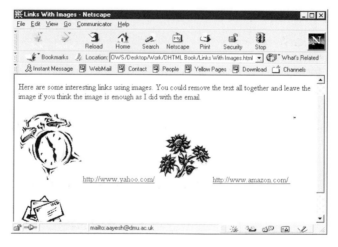

***Fig 7.9** Using the **IMG** tag within <A> tag to make an image link.*

The code I used to create this page is straightforward:

*<P>Here are some interesting links using images. You could remove the text
all together and leave the image if you think the image is enough as I did
with the email. </P>
<P><A HREF="http://www.yahoo.com/">
<IMG SRC="AG00040_.GIF" BORDER=0 WIDTH=128 HEIGHT=142>
http://www.yahoo.com/</A>
<A HREF="http://www.amazon.com/">
<IMG SRC="AG00170_.GIF" BORDER=0 WIDTH=119 HEIGHT=103>*

http://www.amazon.com/ </A></P>
<P><A HREF="mailto:aayesh@dmu.ac.uk">
<IMG SRC="Image5.gif" BORDER=0 WIDTH=92 HEIGHT=94>
</A></P>

Using images navigation toolbar

By using images we can create a toolbar for navigating our web site. It may sound difficult at first but it is much easier than you think and it adds appeal to the web site. It can also be used in combination with frames or JavaScript to create an independent toolbar or for sequential navigation. Here is how it is done.

Decide which web pages you are linking together. Let us assume that we have a links page, a personal details page and a hobbies page.

Choose which pictures, images or graphics are appropriate to these pages.

Now you are ready to use **<IMG>** tag and **<A>** tag to create link images. You could insert these images anywhere within the body of your HTML document depending on where you want them to appear. For example if you want them to appear at the top of the page as in figure 7.10, you should put these links at the beginning of the body of your HTML document.

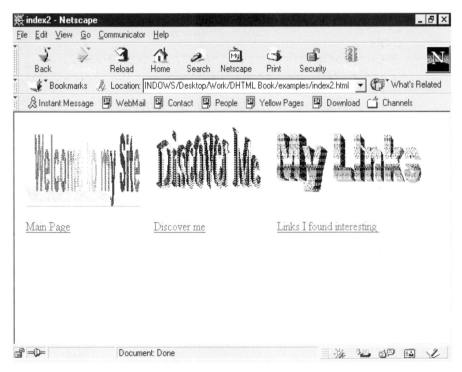

Fig 7.10 *Using images to form menu bar-like navigation links.*

Here is the code you need to produce the above web page:

```
<HTML>
<HEAD>
<TITLE>index2</TITLE>
</HEAD>
<BODY>
<P ALIGN="CENTER"><CENTER><TABLE CELLSPACING=0
BORDER=0 CELLPADDING=7 WIDTH=599>
<TR><TD WIDTH="31%" VALIGN="TOP" HEIGHT=124>
<P><A HREF="Main.html" TARGET="main">
<IMG SRC="WELCOME2.JPG" BORDER=0 WIDTH=165
HEIGHT=108></A></TD>
<TD WIDTH="31%" VALIGN="TOP" HEIGHT=124>
<P><A HREF="DiscoverMe.html" TARGET="main">
<IMG SRC="DISCOVER.JPG" BORDER=0 WIDTH=158
HEIGHT=85></A><BR>
</TD>
<TD WIDTH="38%" VALIGN="TOP" HEIGHT=124>
<P><A HREF="MyLinks.html" TARGET="main">
<IMG SRC="LINKS.JPG" BORDER=0 WIDTH=218
HEIGHT=89></A><BR>
</TD>
</TR>
<TR><TD WIDTH="31%" VALIGN="TOP" HEIGHT=33>
<P><A HREF="Main.html" TARGET="main">Main Page</A>
</TD>
<TD WIDTH="31%" VALIGN="TOP" HEIGHT=33>
<P><A HREF="DiscoverMe.html" TARGET="main">Discover me</A>
</TD>
<TD WIDTH="38%" VALIGN="TOP" HEIGHT=33>
<P><A HREF="MyLinks.html" TARGET="main">Links I found
interesting</A>
</TD>
</TR>
</TABLE>
</CENTER></P>
</BODY>
</HTML>
```

Fig 7.11 *The complete site with menu bar image links.*

Map image

A map image is an image that is used as a map for navigating the web site. The image in the web page shown in figure 7.13 is a map image type. While it is one image, different parts of that image provide a link to different web pages within the site. The benefit of using such a technique is that it provides us with a tool to present our site contents visually instead of just listing them. It acts more like a map for navigation. This map or visual tool makes the site looks more accessible and attractive.

There are two types of map image - server-based and client-based. A server-based map image resides on the server and any access to the links provided by this map image has to go through the server. This may either slow down the navigation between different web pages, or more seriously, if you are connecting through an Internet Service Provider (ISP) it is likely that you would not have such access that allows you to set up a server-based map image. In this respect a client-side map image is more desirable.

Using a map image in your site is going to be through the **IMG** tag. If your map image is server-based you need to use the **ISMAP** attribute; if it is client-based you need to use the **USEMAP** attribute. In the following section we are going to see how to create a client-based map image which will look as impressive as a server-based map image without the worries of putting any scripts on the server-side.

Creating a map image

To create a client-based map image, we need first to prepare the image using an image editor. Paint Shop Pro that is provided with Windows, for example, is suitable (figure 7.12).

Fig 7.12 Using MS Paintshop Pro editor to prepare the map image.

Once we are happy with the image we have to decide which part refers to which page in our site. To make it simple, my image is fancy writing of the page names in my site so it is easy to determine which part of the map image leads to which page. When we have decided on the parts we have to ascertain the coordinates of each part. You need two main co-ordinates for each section of the map image. The first coordinate specifies the upper left corner of a rectangle corresponding to a hyperlink, and the second coordinate specifies the lower right corner. Write down these coordinates for each section of the map image and once you have done this you can move to the second step, which is writing the HTML code to include this map image to produce figure 7.13.

Fig 7.13 The map image in the web page.

The HTML code needed to produce figure 7.13 is:

```
<HTML>
<HEAD>
<TITLE>index using map image</TITLE>
</HEAD>
<BODY>
<P>This is my site index!</P>
<MAP NAME="indeximagemap">
<AREA SHAPE="RECT" COORDS="67,22,133,537"
HREF="Main.html"></A>
<AREA SHAPE="RECT" COORDS="174,112,453,229"
HREF="DiscoverMe.html"></A>
<AREA SHAPE="RECT" COORDS="187,327,445,455"
HREF="MyLinks.html"></A>
</MAP>
<IMG SRC="Mapimage.jpg" USEMAP="#indeximagemap">
</BODY>
</HTML>
```

Note that the map image in figure 7.13 is too big to be viewed all on the screen. This makes the image less effective and so you need to use the image editor to reduce the size of the map image as I have done in figure 7.14.

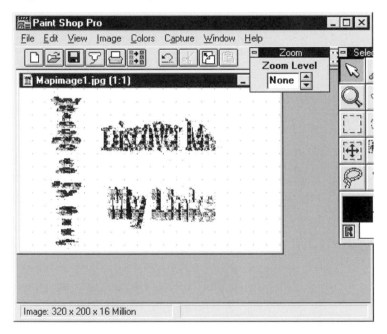

Fig 7.14 *Reducing the size of the map image.*

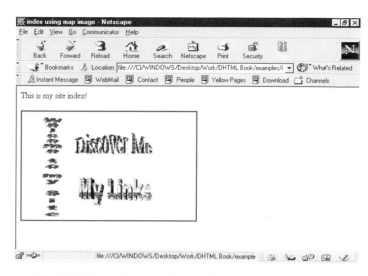

Fig 7.15 *The web page after reducing the image map.*

As we have changed the size of the image we have to change the code to take into account the new coordinates of the different links within the image:

```
<HTML>
<HEAD>
<TITLE>index using map image</TITLE>
</HEAD>
<BODY>
<P>This is my site index! </P>
<MAP NAME="indeximagemap">
<AREA SHAPE="RECT" COORDS="38,5,80,191"
HREF="Main.html"></A>
<AREA SHAPE="RECT" COORDS="99,46,245,71"
HREF="DiscoverMe.html"></A>
<AREA SHAPE="RECT" COORDS="109,121,235,161"
HREF="MyLinks.html"></A>
</MAP>
<IMG SRC="Mapimage1.jpg" USEMAP="#indeximagemap">
</BODY>
</HTML>
```

Note that in the previous two examples there is a **MAP** tag that we use to define the map image.

```
<MAP NAME="indeximagemap">
<AREA SHAPE="RECT" COORDS="38,5,80,191"
HREF="Main.html"></A>
<AREA SHAPE="RECT" COORDS="99,46,245,71"
HREF="DiscoverMe.html"></A>
```

```
<AREA SHAPE="RECT" COORDS="109,121,235,161"
HREF="MyLinks.html"></A>
</MAP>
```

The **AREA** tag is used within the **MAP** tag to define the area of the link in the map image. This tag is very similar to <A> tag. There are, however, the additional attributes of **SHAPE** and **COORDS**. Using a rectangular shape makes it easier for us to identify the coordinates of the area that will be used for each link. Most image editors give the coordinates of different parts of the image which you can use to identify the coordinates of the areas you want to use for links. Note that since I have changed the image size between figures 7.13 and 7.15 I have also had to change the coordinates in the **AREA** tag of each area in the map image.

We still use the **IMG** tag to insert the image but along with the additional **USEMAP** attribute which we use to tell the **IMG** tag that this image is a map image.

```
<IMG SRC="Mapimage1.jpg" USEMAP="#indeximagemap">
```

8
Multimedia Effects

Introduction

You can use different media to present information and enhance the presentation of the web site. These include images, sound, motion images, in other words video and animation, and you can even include 3D virtual reality images. In the previous chapter we considered colour and images. This chapter is devoted to other types of media and the use of relatively more modern technology in web authoring:

- Sound.
- Video.
- The **DYNSRC** attribute.
- The **MARQUEE** tag.
- Using Plug-ins.
- The **EMBED** tag.

File formats

In chapter 7 we saw that images could be stored in a variety of different formats; in a similar way a range of different formats are used for storing sound and video.

The format of the file is usually indicated by the extension of the file, the extension being the two or three letters that follow the file name. As an example, all Word document files have extension doc. And in the previous chapter, the images that are saved in GIF file format have extension gif following the file name and so on.

Sound

Sound is an important form of communication. It can be used in various ways as a means of interaction with the user. You may guide your web site viewers with a voice recorded commentary or share your favourite songs with your viewers. Sound files, therefore, could be:

- Voice.
- Music.
- Reading of text.
- Any noise.

The use of sound can vary from a guiding commentary to a responsive sound or noise. It can also provide a background to set the atmosphere. To do this you need to use the **BGSOUND** tag to play the background sound, but you should be cautious in your choice of sound and the length of playing.

Like images, there are a few sound file formats that can be used:

- Au (filename.au).
- WAV (filename.wav).
- MIDI (filename.mid).

Video

We can include video clips in our web page in the same way images and sound files are included. If you have a video card you can have your favourite clips saved into files. However, you have to save your video files in one of the video formats that are supported by Internet browsers, for example:

- QuickTime MOV (QuickTime format).
- AVI (Windows 95 standard).
- MPEG.

DYNSRC attribute

The **IMG** tag can be used to add a video clip to the web page by using the **DYNSRC** attribute. The following line of code is all you need to do this:

<IMG DYNSRC="videoclipfile.avi" START=mouseover>

If you use this code you will notice that the video clip will start playing when your mouse moves over the clip.

Animation

Animation is an attractive feature to add to a web site. There are three ways to create animation:

- Animated GIF's.
- Java animation applet.
- Macromedia Shockwave.

Animated GIF files can be created using a GIF animator program. You can get a trial version through the Internet or computer art magazine CDs. You can also get animated GIF files from multimedia libraries or by searching the Internet. The MS Word Clip Art libraries contain animated GIF files, a few of which I have used in figure 8.1.

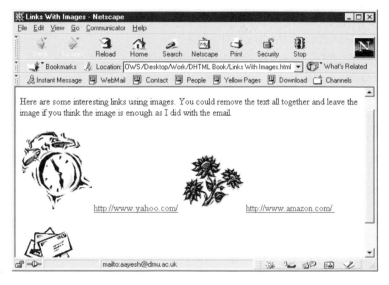

Fig 8.1 *Using animated GIF images as links.*

The code I used to create this page is straightforward:

<P>Here are some interesting links using images. You could remove the text all together and leave the image if you think the image is enough as I did with the email. </P>
<P><A HREF="http://www.yahoo.com/">
<IMG SRC="AG00040_.GIF" BORDER=0 WIDTH=128 HEIGHT=142>
http://www.yahoo.com/</A>
<A HREF="http://www.amazon.com/">
<IMG SRC="AG00170_.GIF" BORDER=0 WIDTH=119 HEIGHT=103>
http://www.amazon.com/ </A></P>
<P><A HREF="mailto:aayesh@dmu.ac.uk">
<IMG SRC="Image5.gif" BORDER=0 WIDTH=92 HEIGHT=94>
</A></P>

I have taken the two animated GIF files which I used here, AG00040_.GIF and AG00170_.GIF, from MS Word. You may like to try some of MS Word clips but make sure that you view your web page with a browser, especially if you are using an authoring tool such as MS Web Authoring Tools in MS Word. In many cases the view of the page in the authoring tools may differ from the page view in a browser. The animated GIF files appear ordinary still images when they are viewed using MS Word or an image editor and as a result the animation will not be noticed.

Java provides a graphics library, which is called the Abstract Window Tool (AWT). However writing your own applets would require long hours of learning and practising Java. Instead you can download applets over the Internet to add that extra touch to your web pages, but you should, however, be aware that using Java applets slows the downloading and viewing of your web page.

MARQUEE tag

If you were wondering how some web pages have moving text here is one way of doing it. By using the **MARQUEE** tag you can add animated text to your web page.

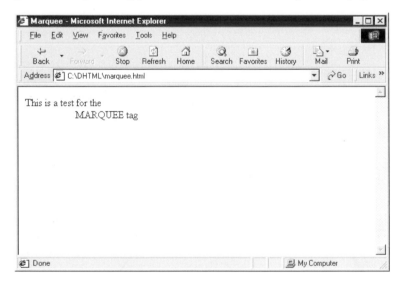

Fig 8.2 Using the *MARQUEE* tag.

Here is the code you need to do this:

```
<HTML>
<HEAD>
<TITLE>Marquee</TITLE>
</HEAD>
<BODY>
This is a test for the
<MARQUEE>MARQUEE tag</MARQUEE>
```

```
</BODY>
</HTML>
```

Unfortunately this tag does not seem to work with Netscape, only with Microsoft Internet Explorer. Compare the following figure with figure 8.2 and you will notice that the text appears as if the **MARQUEE** tag is not there.

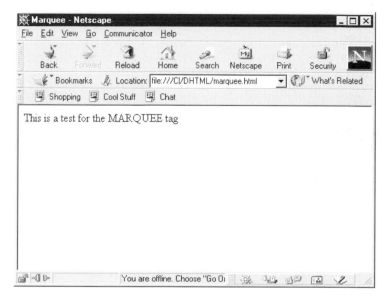

Fig 8.3 *The **MARQUEE** tag does not appear to work with Netscape.*

3D images and virtual reality

There are proposals to develop a Virtual Reality Mark-up Language (VRML) which is derived from HTML. You would need a VRML browser such as Netscape's Live3D. VRML is still under development and its browsers are not as popular as HTML browsers, but as computers become ever more powerful it is an expanding area.

Plug-ins

Plug-ins are software that add more functionality to the browser. As an example, a RealAudio plug-in enables the browser to play audio files. Video clips and some types of animations work along the same lines. Here are some plug-in examples:

- RealAudio real-time audio.
- MidPlug midi player.
- InterVU MPEG player.
- QuickTime for Netscape.

- ViewMovie.
- MovieStar.

Many of these plug-ins are available as shareware which you can download over the Internet. The newer versions of main browsers – for example Netscape Communicator 4.5 – come with their own plug-ins.

EMBED tag

This new tag is used to embed sound and video in web pages.

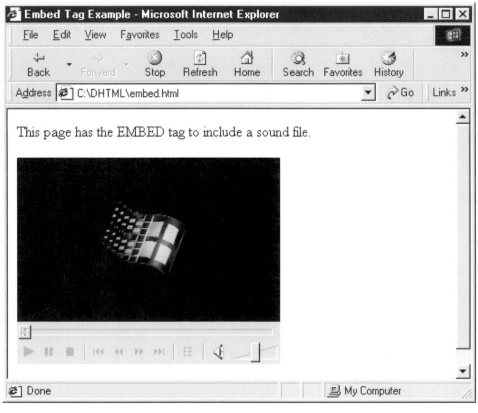

*Fig 8.4 Using the **EMBED** tag to include a sound file.*

The **EMBED** tag can be used within an HTML document like any other tags. The following code is the code I used to include the sound file in figure 8.4:

```
<HTML>
<HEAD>
<TITLE>Embed Tag Example</TITLE>
</HEAD>
```

```
<BODY>
<P>This page has the EMBED tag to include a sound file.</P>
<P>
<EMBED SRC="song03-1.mid"><P>
</BODY>
</HTML>
```

BGSOUND tag

The **BGSOUND** tag allows us to add background music to our web pages. The advisability of doing this obviously depends on the type of web page we are constructing. If our site is about music or romantic holidays it might be nice to set the scene. **BGSOUND** is very simple to set up:

<BGSOUND SRC="song03-1.mid" LOOP=1>

Notice, however, that the music will play as soon as the page is downloaded. If you want the music to play for longer or be repeated you can use the **LOOP** attribute, setting it to the number of times you want the music to be played. It is especially useful when you are playing a short extract of music, but be careful as over use may irritate viewers.

9

Background and Layout

Introduction

It is important in designing our web site to consider the layout of the pages. In this chapter we are going to look at the issues relating to the layout design starting with examples from existing web sites. We shall also cover the overview planning of web pages, extending to:

- The font.
- The use of multimedia effects.
- Links.

And we shall conclude with some tips on getting resources for our web site through the Internet.

Examples of layout from existing sites

As you may see in figure 9.1, each page has a background and elements to distribute over that background.

Fig 9.1 *Image-based background.*

Fig 9.2 *Front elements over figure 9.1 background.*

The balance between the background and the front elements should be maintained to produce an attractive site. This balance covers colours, fonts, contents structure, and the amount of contents presented. Figure 9.3 shows a crowded web page.

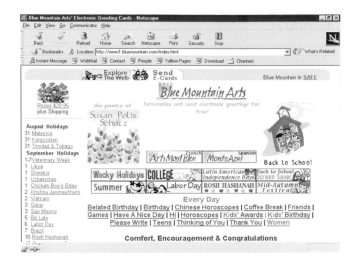

Fig 9.3 *Crowded web page.*

You may like to count how many links, images, headers and other elements appear in figure 9.3. These crowded elements make the page difficult and uncomfortable to view. It is possible to include many links and other front elements to a web page in a more organised form but it is not really advisable. The organisation of the front elements is the main way of making the pages easier for the viewer to follow. Figure 9.4 shows a better organised web page even though the page is still too crowded.

Fig. 9.4 *Better organised web page elements.*

Overview planning

It is important to know the overview of your site before you start constructing it. The things you have to decide are:

- Is it going to be one page or several pages?
- Do I need an index or will there just be sequential pages?
- How will these pages follow and be related to each other?

To help you answer these questions you may use storyboarding. Storyboarding is a graphical representation of scenes or screens. Before you start implementing your site you have to draw on paper how you want it to look, and to do this there are two steps you should follow.

Think of each screen or HTML document in your site as a movie scene. Then decide what that scene should contain and how it will appear. Drawing a box or rectangle on paper for each scene will help in constraining you to a screen. In the box you can draw or write what is going to go there.

Then decide where that scene fits and how it links to other documents in your site. You can use arrows to link between your scenes.

This completes your storyboard and you can start implementing your site with a predetermined overview of what it will look like and how it will function.

Background planning

It is a good idea to start planning the background first, before worrying about what is going on top. Try to make the background as simple as you can - using clear colours. White is the usual background colour but there is nothing to prevent you from using yellow, pink, sky blue or even black. Try to avoid colours such as green, red and dark blue as they are midway between dark (cool) colours and bright (warm) colours. With middle colours you will find it difficult to find appropriate font colours.

A graphical pattern needs to be kept simple too, as you do not want the background pattern to take over the front elements. What I said about colours applies again here. If you are using pictures you need to consider both the colours and details of the picture. Too many details in the picture will distract the viewer and leave a feeling of overcrowding; too many colours will be confusing and may obscure the front elements. As a general rule use a pattern-based image if you are going to use a background image. If your web page is a business web page, that image could be your company logo. However if you are using a business logo try to fade the colours first.

Whatever your decision about the background try to maintain a standardised look for your web site. Avoid using too many colours, patterns and pictures. Choose your background carefully and then use it as a theme through your web site unless there is a strong reason to do otherwise.

Front elements

The front elements are text, images and links. Organising these elements on the page is an important element of web design. It might be a good idea to look at many different web sites and jot down the points that you like and dislike about each site. You will learn a lot from this practice and get more ideas for your own site.

Font and structure

The use of a suitable font is important in stressing the structural boundaries between the different parts of a document. It is like using a drawing pen in a watercolour picture to highlight the boundaries between different parts of the painting which share, to some extent, the same texture. Therefore fonts have to be chosen with care.

First start by identifying your headings or main topics covered in your document. If you are working on your personal web site, for example, your main topics may include hobbies, your sports club, your profession and so on. Under each of these topics or headings you may have some descriptive text or links to related web sites. Now decide which font and colour these headings will take. If you are using **H1** for your page heading and **H2** for the subheadings on that page then try to use that style in all your pages within the site. And try to use the same colour.

When you choose the font size for the text that comes under these headings you have to take into account the distribution of text on your page and the relevance to your headings. For example, you should use a bigger font size for the headings, but you should avoid crowding your web pages with big fonts that limit the amount of text visible on a page. In fact you should try to keep each of your web pages within one page or one screen as much as possible. In general the best way to judge the font, colour and distribution of your text within web pages is by considering yourself to be the viewer.

Multimedia

Using multimedia effects adds a more professional touch and makes web pages more attractive to view. However the use of multimedia effects requires resources, for example it takes time to load images. If you are using too many multimedia components you may be imposing heavily on the viewer resources and that may lead the viewer to cancel the loading of your page to look somewhere else. This was not your intention when you decided to use multimedia in your web page.

If you are going to use multimedia, study carefully your resources and your viewers. This is similar to market research. If your target audience are busy organisations it is unlikely they will wait for many images to download on one page. Also background sound may not appeal to them, as it would do holiday seekers. While if your web page is about games, your viewers are going to be interested in images from those games and any sound tracks that come with them.

Market research may be successful to some extent but there are general points you have to consider. Your first objective is to attract the viewers or Internet users to look at your page. Make the first page relatively simple but inviting, as it is an opening statement of the site. Make sure the links to other parts of your site are presented nicely and clearly. Remember images, especially JPEG, take less time to download than animation. There is no harm in using some images to present your links or to give samples of the link contents. If you are going to do so, it is worth checking the size of the images you are using. You may edit or cut these images to make the file size smaller. It is good idea to limit the animations to short and small files. Try to have the video clips in a separate file so they run only if the user wants them to. As for sound, be careful; it is very effective if it is used appropriately but it can be annoying if it goes on for too long or is too loud. In all cases consider the size of the files and the number of the components on each page; you should balance between the two to keep the downloading of each page to a reasonable rate. Always feel free to edit your files to make them smaller or to create snap shots that need less time to download.

Links

There are two types of links you should consider in your web site design: internal and external. By internal links we mean the links between different web pages on the same site. External links are our links to web sites other than our own. As an example, your personal site may contain three web pages: main page, links and hobbies page and a CV page. You may also create another site for your business that may contain various web pages depending on your business. It would be useful to have an external link between your two sites.

Internal links are very important in deciding the layout of your web pages and your site as a whole. Internal links are used to break long texts into smaller chunks that are easier to view and digest. This is the main principle behind the hypertext idea which is central to HTML.

Find and collect resources

As you develop your web site you will need some resources (for example images, audio files and so on). While some resource libraries may be expensive to buy, producing your own resources would require equipment such as a scanner, photo editors and so on, as well as the technical knowledge to use them. There is an even better way to get unlimited material for use in developing your site: use the Internet itself, where much resource material is available free and is often more up to date than resource libraries. Figures 9.5 and 9.6 show two sites where you can download some useful resources.

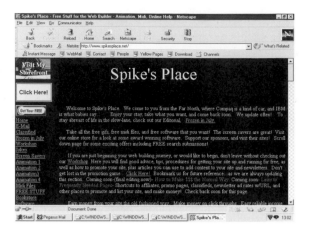

Fig 9.5 *Spikes web page with lots of animations and midi files.*

Fig 9.6 *The Groove Box web page with lots of free resources by email.*

Overall presentation and web publishing

Once you have decided how you are going to develop your site and gathered your resources it is time to put them together to produce your site. Here are some tips to keep your important overall presentation effective.

Keep consistency between your web pages as much as you can. This applies to colour, fonts and background. For example, if you started with font **H1** for the headings it would be sensible to keep using that font for all your headings on all of your pages.

Use colours wisely and economically, as too many colours make pages difficult to read.

Images are more effective if they have relevance to the web page content, and are of appropriate size in comparison to that content. For example, using some sized images of local interests with a related description of the place of interest (such as a city hall picture next to a paragraph which describes the city hall), greatly enhances the web site.

Make sure that internal links are relatively addressed as it makes it easier to move your site from one directory to another. Make sure also, that all your web pages are present in your directory when you move the site to your area on the web server or your internet provider server. Nothing is more disappointing than trying to move to another page in a site and not finding that page. If some of your pages are still under construction try to replace it with an alternative web page that indicates this and contains some information about when the finished version will be available.

10
Dynamic HTML and Style Sheets

Introduction

Dynamic HTML or DHTML is popular in web page design and authoring. It simply refers to the increasing use of animated HTML in which the responses to the user actions come directly from the HTML code on the client machine rather than from the hosting server. This animation is possible through the use of new HTML tags and scripting. In this chapter we will look at the DHTML aspects that extend HTML with references to the coming chapters. In the following chapters each aspect of DHTML will be explored in detail. These aspects are:

- Cascading Style Sheets (CSS).
- Layers.
- Document Object Model (DOM).
- Dynamic positioning.
- Dynamic contents.
- Data binding.
- Downloadable fonts.
- Scripting.

You can use the headings in this chapter as keywords in searching the Internet for more information about DHTML as they represent the core of DHTML.

Cascading Style Sheets (CSS)

Style Sheets were one of the first features of DHTML to be developed. As a result the two main browsers Netscape and Microsoft IE support style sheets which are usually referred to as Cascading Style Sheets (CSS). These are covered in chapter 11.

Layers

Layers are an invention of Netscape and use the **LAYER** tag. They can be implemented using CSS and they are in principle the alternative to frames. Layers differ from frames in the sense that layers can be positioned on exact locations on the screen rather than leaving the positioning for the browser. Layers will be described in further detail in chapter 12.

Document Object Model (DOM)

The Document Object Model (DOM) was developed by both Microsoft and Netscape, although it goes back to the early specifications of HTML when JavaScript was introduced. However, the implementation of DOM in these two browsers is slightly different, resulting in some incompatibility between the two. Understanding DOM will enable us to see how the web browsers work and will give us a better perception of how the different elements of a web page can be accessed and manipulated to our wishes. This is covered in chapter 13.

Dynamic positioning

Dynamic positioning is concerned with moving the contents of the page (elements) from one position to another. This is different from animation in the sense that the user may not notice the positioning but it gives control over where the contents are displayed. This is important when are you presenting different blocks of contents in relation to each other. It also complements the usage of dynamic contents. This is covered in chapter 14.

Dynamic contents

Dynamic contents covers the aspects of moving, adding or hiding some of the page contents after the page is loaded and displayed. In chapter 15 we shall see through an example how to alternate between two pages in response to a user's moving mouse. In dynamic positioning and dynamic contents we shall need to use some scripting that mainly relies on DOM.

Scripting

Scripting is covered in chapter 17. There are two types of scripting, client-side and server-side. DHTML is concerned with client-side scripting that reduces the processing time. In other words the time to download the site will be less because the scripting will be executed on the client-side. As a result the site control will be done from the client-side rather than from the server-side, as is the case of CGI scripting, the earlier technology used in controlling web sites.

Data binding

Data binding applies the principle of DHTML in dealing with data, allowing us to handle data at the client end. This includes asking questions or requesting information from the user, changing elements on our document including values and appearances, and getting results from an associated text file or a database. This is all done without the need to go back to the server.

Downloadable fonts

The idea of downloadable fonts is to enable us to use the fonts that we like in order to enhance our text and to package these fonts with our web pages. When the viewer downloads our web page he will download the fonts within the document and view the text in the fonts that we have chosen. Data binding and downloadable fonts are advanced DHTML features which we shall look at briefly in chapter 18.

Technology and techniques

We have to be clear about the difference between Cascading Style Sheets (CSS), dynamic positioning and scripting, in terms of which one is a technology and which one is a technique. DHTML writers do not usually distinguish between DHTML technology and techniques but I feel that doing so will help in understanding the coming chapters.

In summary, the key features of DHTML technology are:

- Style sheets.
- Layers.
- Document Object Model (DOM).
- Dynamic positioning.
- Dynamic contents.
- Data binding.
- Downloadable fonts.

The techniques we use to deploy these technologies vary depending on the tools we use. For example, layers, as we shall see in chapter 12, can be defined using the

LAYER tag or using CSS layers. CSS, layers and DOM contain the techniques that we shall see in other components of DHTML such as dynamic positioning and contents. The **DIV** tag, for example, is a technique which is used to apply styles as we shall see in chapter 11, but also can be used in dynamic positioning as we shall see in chapter 14.

Using the head of the page

You may have been wondering what is the use of the head section of a web page, defined by **<HEAD>** ... **</HEAD>** tag, besides containing the title of the page. From this point forward the **HEAD** section of the web page document will be used. It includes style definitions, scripts and so on.

It is important to appreciate that all the parts that will not appear directly on the display of the web page may be included in the **HEAD** section. However these parts may be named within some tags in the **BODY** section of the document.

11
Cascading Style Sheets

Introduction

Style sheets are based on the use of the **STYLE** tag, which allows us to define new styles, for example fonts, to use on our web page. Style sheets or Cascading Style Sheets (CSS), as DHTML authors usually refer to them, allow us also to define blocks of content. Once these are defined we can control their position on the web page, that is we can cascade them. We shall see more about controlling the positioning of blocks of content when we come to dynamic positioning in chapter 14.

In addition CSS replaces the need to use Java scripting to change the styles of the web page. In other words what we can do using the **STYLE** tag can be done using Java script within the context of the Document Object Model (DOM), which is covered in chapter 13.

In this chapter however we shall learn how to write CSS to define new styles, and how to apply these styles to different parts of our web page to add a special touch. We are going to look at:

- The **STYLE** tag.
- The **DIV** tag.
- The **SPAN** tag.

STYLE tag

We shall begin our look at CSS with the **STYLE** tag in a simple format. The **STYLE** tag is used to define a style which may be applied to one or more blocks of content at any time later on in the document.

We should not confuse the **STYLE** tag with the **STYLE** attribute which we shall see later on in this chapter. The **STYLE** tag is a tag within which a style definition is included. The **STYLE** attribute is a new attribute that is added to some existing HTML tags to allow us to change some of style properties of those tags.

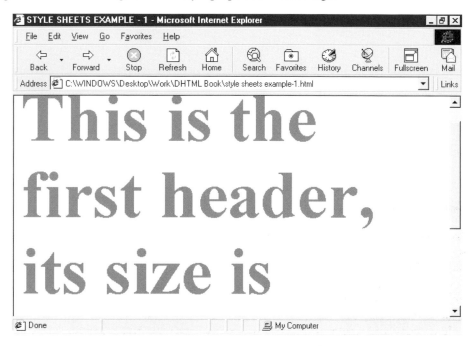

Fig 11.1 *Using the **STYLE** tag to change the **H1** font size.*

The code that I used to change the size of the first header, in other words the **H1** tag, is as follows:

```
<HTML>
<TITLE>STYLE SHEETS EXAMPLE - 1</TITLE>
<STYLE>
H1 {COLOR:red; FONT-SIZE:72pt}
</STYLE>
<BODY>
<H1>This is the first header, its size is changed using CSS</H1>
</BODY>
</HTML>
```

Notice that I have also changed the colour of the header. This does not appear in the screen dump but if you try the code you will notice the colour change.

Fig.11.2 *Changing the font style of **H1**.*

I modified the code which I used in the previous example (figure 11.2) using the **FONT-STYLE** attribute of **H1** tag within the tag:

```
<HTML>
<TITLE>STYLE SHEETS EXAMPLE - 2</TITLE>
<STYLE>
H1 {COLOR:red; FONT-SIZE:72pt; FONT-STYLE:italic}
</STYLE>
<BODY>
<H1>This is the first header with italic style</H1>
</BODY>
</HTML>
```

STYLE attribute within the BODY tag

The **STYLE** attribute can be used within the **BODY** tag to apply the chosen style to the whole document. Figure 11.3 shows an example using the **STYLE** attribute within the **BODY** tag.

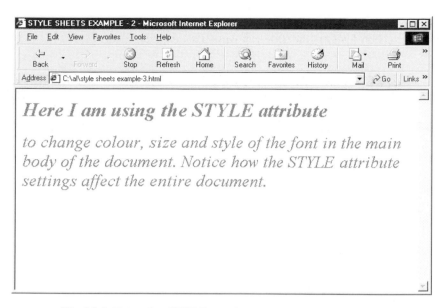

Fig 11.3 *Using the **STYLE** attribute in Internet Explorer.*

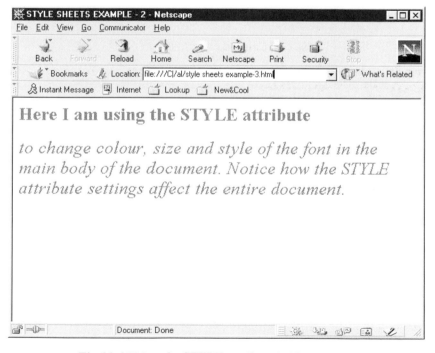

Fig 11.4 *Using the **STYLE** attribute in Netscape.*

The code I used to produce figures 11.3 and 11.4 is:

```
<HTML>
<TITLE>STYLE SHEETS EXAMPLE - 2</TITLE>
<BODY STYLE="COLOR: red; FONT-SIZE:20pt;
FONT-STYLE:italic">
<H1> Here I am using the STYLE attribute </H1>
to change colour, size and style of the font in the main body of the document.
Notice how the STYLE attribute settings affect the entire document.
</BODY>
</HTML>
```

Notice the difference between using the **STYLE** tag and the **STYLE** attribute. We can control our style better with the **STYLE** tag and can apply the style we have chosen to the whole document using the **STYLE** attribute. However the behaviour of the **STYLE** attribute varies between Netscape and Explorer as figures 11.3 and 11.4 show.

External style sheets

Style sheets can be placed into a text file separated from the web site document code. To do this we take all the styles we defined with the **STYLE** tag and include them in a text file with the extension CSS. This technique is helpful when we have a number of styles which are used frequently in our web site. It saves rewriting them every time we need to use them as well as making it easier to debug the web pages and CSS. We shall be discussing debugging in chapter 16. In this section, however, we shall look at using a separate file to collect our style sheets together.

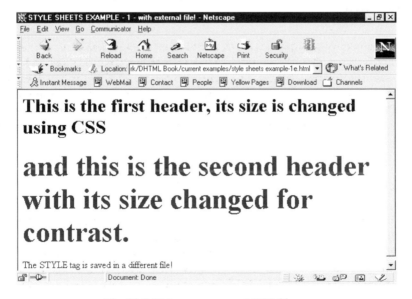

Fig 11.5 Using an external CSS file.

The web page shown in figure 11.5 was produced using an external CSS file. The code that is saved in the external file is:

```
<STYLE>
H1 {COLOR:red; FONT-SIZE:12pt}
H2 {COLOR:blue; FONT-SIZE:36pt}
</STYLE>
```

I called this file "*cssexample-1e.css*". The extension '.css' is important for the browser to identify the file that contains Cascaded Style Sheets (CSS). The HTML document is the same as in the previous example except that I have used the **LINK** tag to link the CSS text file within the HTML document.

```
<HTML>
<HEAD>
<TITLE>STYLE SHEETS EXAMPLE - 1 - with external file!</TITLE>
<LINK REL="stylesheet" TYPE="text/css" HREF="cssexample-1e.css">
</HEAD>
<BODY>
<H1>This is the first header, its size is changed using CSS</H1>
<H2>and this is the second header with its size changed for contrast.</H2>
The STYLE tag is saved in a different file!
</body>
</HTML>
```

Applying style

There are many ways to apply a style to a section or a word. To do so we need to use additional tags to the **STYLE** tag: the **BLOCKQUOTE** tag, the **DIV** tag and the **SPAN** tag. The main difference between these tags and the **STYLE** tag is that these tags are used within the body of the HTML document. The **STYLE** tag is used to define a style, where **DIV** and **SPAN** are used to apply a style to a particular part of the document. To do this we use the **STYLE** attribute in these two tags which should not be confused with the **STYLE** tag.

BLOCKQUOTE tag

The **BLOCKQUOTE** tag is an effective tag to be used in conjunction with the **STYLE** tag. As the tag name may indicate, the **BLOCKQUOTE** tag is used in handling a block of content (text); therefore it is useful in applying a style to a block of content. By using the **STYLE** tag, we can define a style for the **BLOCKQUOTE** tag, which will be applied whenever the **BLOCKQUOTE** tag is used. The following example shown in figure 11.6 illustrates this.

Fig 11.6 *Using the **BLOCKQUOTE** tag in applying style to a block of text.*

The code that I used to produce this style is:

```
<HTML>
<HEAD>
<TITLE>STYLE SHEETS EXAMPLE - 5</TITLE>
</HEAD>
<STYLE>
H1 {TEXT-ALIGN:center; BACKGROUND:black;
COLOR:white; FONT-SIZE:36pt; FONT-STYLE:italic}
BLOCKQUOTE {MARGIN-LEFT:100px; MARGIN-RIGHT:100px;
COLOR:blue; FONT-SIZE:12pt; FONT-FAMILY:arial}
</STYLE>
<BODY>
<H1>This is my stylish header</H1>
<BLOCKQUOTE>
Hello! This is an example showing you how to use the BLOCKQUOTE tag to
specify margins.
</BLOCKQUOTE>
</BODY>
</HTML>
```

You should not confuse the **BLOCKQUOTE** tag with the **DIV** tag. We define the style of the **BLOCKQUOTE** tag using the **STYLE** tag, and the **DIV** tag enables us to break the document into several sections. Then we have the choice of applying styles defined using the **STYLE** tag or defining each **DIV** section style separately using the **STYLE** attribute within the **DIV** tag.

DIV tag

The **DIV** tag is used to divide the body of an HTML document into sections. It does not do much on its own. You may not even notice its effects on the presentation of the page. As an example, I have used the **DIV** tag in the web page in figure 11.7.

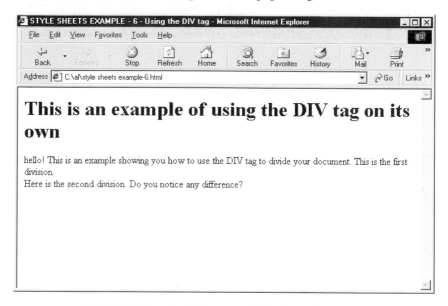

Fig 11.7 *Using the **DIV** tag to divide the web page.*

The code that is used in this example is:

```
<HTML>
<HEAD>
<TITLE> STYLE SHEETS EXAMPLE - 6 - Using the DIV tag </TITLE>
</HEAD>
<BODY>
<H1> This is an example of using the DIV tag on its own</H1>
<DIV>
hello! This is an example showing you how to use the DIV tag to divide your
document. This is the first division.
</DIV>
<DIV>
Here is the second division. Do you notice any difference?
</DIV>
</BODY>
</HTML>
```

Note that the use of the **DIV** tag hardly alters the way the document looks. Now let us use the **STYLE** attribute within the **DIV** tag. The result can be seen in Figure 11.8.

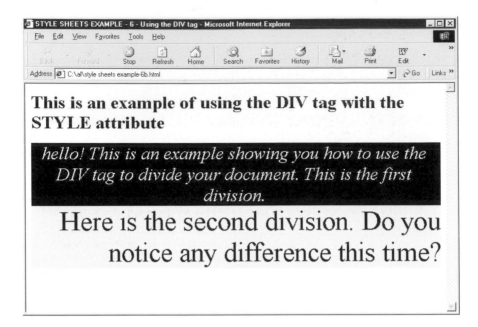

The code that is used in this example is:

```
<HTML>
<HEAD>
<TITLE>STYLE SHEETS EXAMPLE - 6 - Using the DIV tag</TITLE>
</HEAD>
<BODY>
<H1>This is an example of using the DIV tag with the STYLE
attribute</H1>
<DIV STYLE="TEXT-ALIGN:center; BACKGROUND:black;
COLOR:white; FONT-SIZE:24pt; FONT-STYLE:italic">
hello! This is an example showing you how to use the DIV tag to divide your
document.  This is the first division.
</DIV>
<DIV STYLE="TEXT-ALIGN:right; BACKGROUND:yellow;
COLOR:black; FONT-SIZE:36pt; FONT-STYLE:bold">
Here is the second division.  Do you notice any difference this time?
</DIV>
</BODY>
</HTML>
```

SPAN tag

The **SPAN** tag allows us to apply a style to any part of the body of the document, even to one word. The **SPAN** and **DIV** tags are the backbone of style sheets technology and we shall see them again in dynamic positioning, in chapter 14.

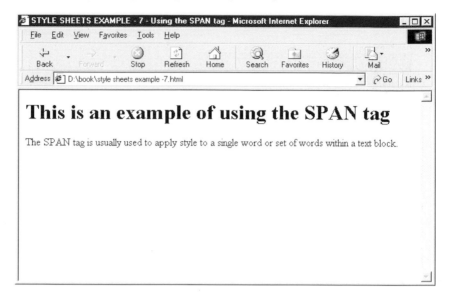

Fig 11.9 Using the SPAN tag on its own.

You can recreate figure 11.9 using the following code:

```
<HTML>
<HEAD>
<TITLE>STYLE SHEETS EXAMPLE - 7 - Using the SPAN tag</TITLE>
</HEAD>
<BODY>
<H1> This is an example of using the SPAN tag</H1>
<SPAN> The SPAN tag is usually used to</SPAN>
<SPAN>apply style</SPAN>
<SPAN> to a single word or set of words within a text block.</SPAN>
</BODY>
</HTML>
```

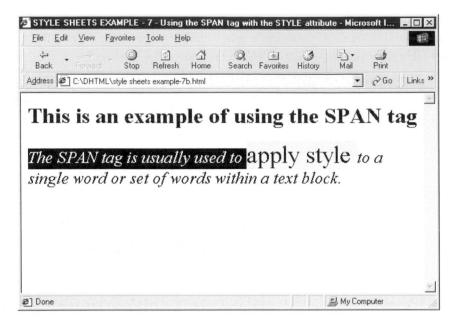

Fig 11.10 *Using the **SPAN** tag to apply different styles to set of words.*

I produced figure 11.10 using the following code:

```
<HTML>
<HEAD>
<TITLE>
STYLE SHEETS EXAMPLE - 7 - Using the SPAN tag with the STYLE
attribute
 </TITLE>
</HEAD>
<BODY>
<H1>This is an example of using the SPAN tag</H1>
<SPAN STYLE="TEXT-ALIGN: center; BACKGROUND:black;
COLOR:white; FONT-SIZE:24; FONT-STYLE:italic">
The SPAN tag is usually used to
</SPAN>
<SPAN STYLE= "TEXT-ALIGN:right; BACKGROUND:yellow;
COLOR:black; FONT-SIZE:36; FONT-STYLE:bold">
 apply style
</SPAN>
<SPAN STYLE= "TEXT-ALIGN:left; BACKGROUND:white;
COLOR:black; FONT-SIZE:24; FONT-STYLE:italic">
to a single word or set of words within a text block.
</SPAN>
</BODY>
</HTML>
```

Notice how the **SPAN** tag is used in a similar way to the **DIV** tag, but does not define blocks. In other words we can include span within a sentence without forcing the line to break. This allows us to apply different styles to parts of a block of text.

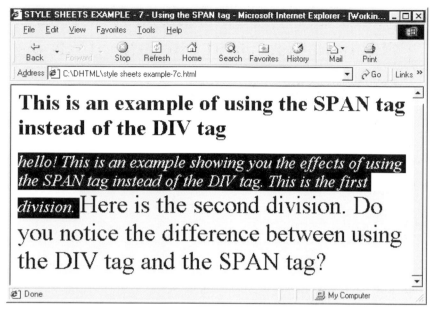

Fig 11.11 Using the SPAN tag instead of the DIV tag.

The code that I used to produce figure 11.11 using the **SPAN** tag is as follows:

```
<HTML>
<HEAD>
<TITLE>STYLE SHEETS EXAMPLE - 7 - Using the SPAN tag </TITLE>
</HEAD>
<BODY>
<H1>This is an example of using the SPAN tag instead of the DIV
tag</H1>
<SPAN STYLE="TEXT-ALIGN:center; BACKGROUND:black;
COLOR:white; FONT-SIZE:24; FONT-STYLE:italic">
hello! This is an example showing you the effects of using the SPAN tag
instead of the DIV tag.  This is the first division.
</SPAN>
<SPAN STYLE="TEXT-ALIGN:right; BACKGROUND:yellow;
COLOR:black; FONT-SIZE:36; FONT-STYLE:bold">
Here is the second division.  Do you notice the difference between using the
DIV tag and the SPAN tag?
</SPAN>
</BODY>
</HTML>
```

By using the three tags, **STYLE**, **DIV** and **SPAN**, we can produce an endless combination of styles in our documents. Even though I used only text in my examples, these tags can be used with images and links as well. In fact, if you are going to use DHTML in authoring your web site it is advisable to divide your contents using the **DIV** tags before using CSS or layers. We shall discuss layers in the next chapter.

12
Layers

Introduction

Layers are usually associated with Netscape because of the **LAYER** tag which is a Netscape innovation. The easy way to understand layers is to think of them as flexible frames. Frames, which we studied in chapter 4, are strict in the way they are displayed, as their size, place and number are pre-defined. Layers, however, can be controlled individually by showing or hiding each layer as desired. In addition, the position where these layers are displayed can be fixed independently from other layers or related to other layers.

In this chapter we are going to look at the use of layers and their positioning. This includes defining layers, absolute positioning, relative positioning and some examples of using layers. Two main ways of defining layers will be discussed:

- The **LAYER** tag.
- CSS layers.

In addition we are going to look at two new tags:

- The **ILAYER** tag.
- The **NOLAYER** tag.

Defining layers

There are two main ways of defining layers. We can either use CSS syntax or the **LAYER** tag. If we use CSS syntax the **STYLE** tag is used to define the layer's style and the **DIV** and **SPAN** tags are used to apply that style to the layer content. We call this type of layer a CSS layer. The alternative way of defining layers is to use the **LAYER** and **ILAYER** tags, which we shall cover in detail later within this chapter. Note that we can only use the **LAYER** tag, and consequently the **ILAYER** tag, with Netscape Navigator v4.0 or later versions.

Before exploring the wonderful world of layers we need to do some preparation. We need to have a plan before we start defining our layers. How many layers do we require? What is the relationship between these layers? Remember that layers are similar to frames with one important difference, we have the flexibility to position them anywhere on the screen. As we shall see in chapter 14, layers are often used for positioning contents. Positioning can be either absolute or relative and we have to understand these two concepts of positioning to be able to progress further, in particular how to use one of the essential features of DHTML technology, dynamic positioning.

Absolute and relative positioning

Absolute positioning refers to a fixed positioning of a layer or component regardless of other components. Relative positioning refers to a positioning of a layer or component with reference to other components.

Absolute and relative positioning are important DHTML concepts that will appear again when we discuss dynamic positioning in chapter 14. In this chapter, however, we shall see how they are used with the **LAYER** and **ILAYER** tags, and how these two types of positioning distinguish between the two layers.

LAYER tag

As layers are Netscape-exclusive you may not use them often. However, it is important to know how to use them since the Netscape browser is widely used. In this section we are going to look at the **LAYER** tag within examples of both types of positioning.

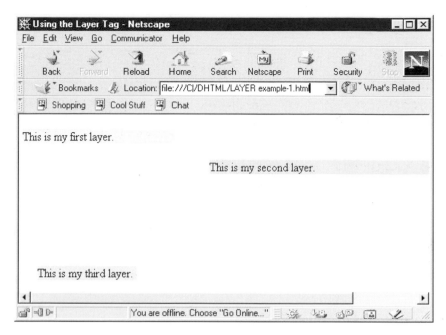

Fig 12.1 *Using the **LAYER** tag.*

The following code is used to produce figure 12.1:

```
<HTML>
<HEAD>
<TITLE>Using the Layer Tag</TITLE>
</HEAD>
<BODY>
<LAYER ID=layer1 TOP=20PT LEFT=5PT, BGCOLOR="YELLOW"
WIDTH=200>
This is my first layer.
</LAYER>
<LAYER ID=layer2 TOP=60PT LEFT=250PT BGCOLOR=skyblue
WIDTH=400>
This is my second layer.
</LAYER>
<LAYER ID=layer3 TOP=200PT LEFT=25PT BGCOLOR=PINK>
This is my third layer.
</LAYER>
</BODY>
</HTML>
```

Take a portion of figure 12.1 code:

```
<LAYER ID=layer1 TOP=20PT LEFT=5PT, BGCOLOR="YELLOW"
WIDTH=200>
```

Notice the following in using the **LAYER** tag:

- There is an **ID** attribute which identifies the layer so that it can be used as a reference to the layer within other parts of code such as JavaScript code.
- There are coordinate attributes which define the positioning of the layer.
- There are other attributes related to the style of the layer itself such as the **BGCOLOR** attribute to set the background colour and the **WIDTH** attribute to set the width of the layer.

ILAYER tag

The **ILAYER** tag is designed to define relatively positioned layers. We use the **ILAYER** tag to implement relatively positioned layers, which are referred to as inflow layers. Figures 12.1 and 12.2 show the difference between using the **LAYER** and **ILAYER** tags. Note that to show the variation I removed the **TOP**, **LEFT** and **WIDTH** attributes.

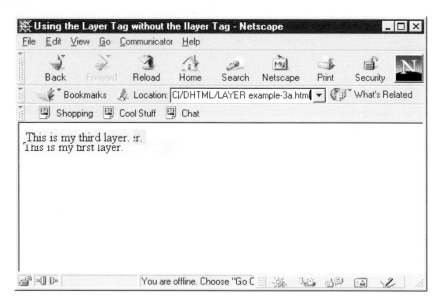

*Fig 12.2 Using the **ILAYER** tag for relatively positioned layers.*

The code that I used to produce this page is very similar to the code I used in the **LAYER** tag example:

```
<HTML>
<HEAD>
<TITLE>Using the Layer Tag without the Ilayer Tag</TITLE>
</HEAD>
<BODY>
<LAYER ID=layer1 TOP=20PT LEFT=5PT, BGCOLOR="YELLOW"
```

```
WIDTH=200>
This is my first layer.
</LAYER>
<LAYER ID=layer2 BGCOLOR=skyblue>
This is my second layer.
</LAYER>
<LAYER ID=layer3 BGCOLOR=PINK>
This is my third layer.
</LAYER>
</BODY>
</HTML>
```

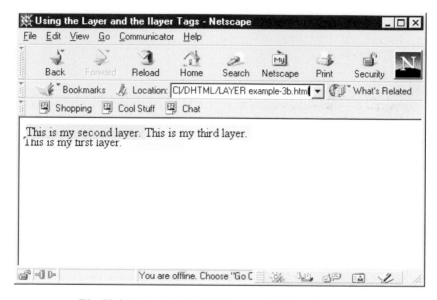

Fig 12.3 *Using the ILAYER tag with three layers.*

In figure 12.3 I used the **ILAYER** tag and the third layer has moved to fit next to the second layer. The code to do this is:

```
<HTML>
<HEAD>
<TITLE>Using the Layer and the Ilayer Tags</TITLE>
</HEAD>
<BODY>
<LAYER ID=layer1 TOP=20PT LEFT=5PT, BGCOLOR="YELLOW"
WIDTH=200>
This is my first layer.
</LAYER>
<ILAYER ID=layer2 BGCOLOR=skyblue>
This is my second layer.
```

```
</ILAYER>
<ILAYER ID=layer3 BGCOLOR=PINK>
This is my third layer.
</ILAYER>
</BODY>
</HTML>
```

Note that this code is almost identical to the code I used in figure 12.1 except that the **ILAYER** tag is used in the second and third layers. In addition, notice how the inner layers start from the top of the browser window and then follow each other regardless to other layers. If you want inner layers to start from another position you have to use coordinate attributes to force it as it is shown in figure 12.4.

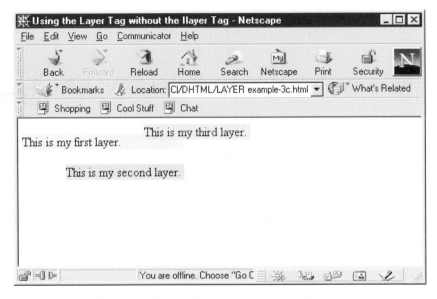

Fig. 12.4 *Positioning inner layers explicitly.*

The code I used in figure 12.4 with explicit coordinates for the second layer is:

```
<HTML>
<HEAD>
<TITLE>Using the Layer Tag without the Ilayer Tag</TITLE>
</HEAD>
<BODY>
<LAYER ID=layer1 TOP=20PT LEFT=5PT BGCOLOR="YELLOW"
WIDTH=200>
This is my first layer.
</LAYER>
<ILAYER ID=layer2 TOP=50PT LEFT=50PT BGCOLOR=skyblue>
This is my second layer.
</ILAYER>
```

```
<ILAYER ID=layer3 BGCOLOR=PINK>
This is my third layer.
</ILAYER>
</BODY>
</HTML>
```

Once explicit coordinates are used, the behaviour of inner layers may not be what you expect. It is always a good practice to try your ideas before continuing to build your site.

CSS layers

It is not necessary to use the **LAYER** tag when you want to build layers. You can use what you have learnt in the Cascading Style Sheets chapter to build layers. These are called CSS layers.

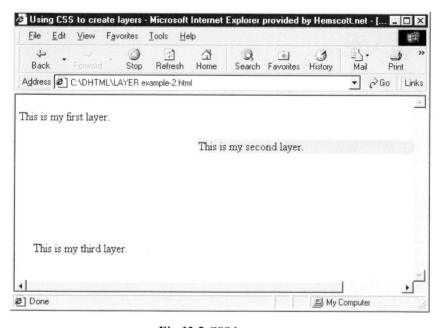

Fig 12.5 CSS layers.

The code for CSS layers is:

```
<HTML>
<HEAD>
<TITLE>Using CSS to create layers</TITLE>
</HEAD>
<STYLE TYPE="text/css">
<!--
#layer1 {POSITION:absolute; TOP:20px; LEFT:5px;
```

```
BACKGROUND-COLOR:"YELLOW"; WIDTH:200}
#layer2 {POSITION:absolute; TOP:60px; LEFT:250px;
BACKGROUND-COLOR:"skyblue"; WIDTH:400}
#layer3 {POSITION:absolute; TOP:200px; LEFT: 25px;
BACKGROUND-COLOR:"pink"}
-->
</STYLE>
<BODY>
<DIV ID=layer1>
This is my first layer.
</DIV>
<DIV ID=layer2>
This is my second layer.
</DIV>
<DIV ID=layer3>
This is my third layer.
</DIV>
</BODY>
</HTML>
```

In CSS layers code note how we used the **STYLE** tag to define the layers:

```
<STYLE TYPE="text/css">
<!--
#layer1 {POSITION:absolute; TOP:20px; LEFT:5px;
BACKGROUND-COLOR:"YELLOW"; WIDTH:200}
#layer2 {POSITION:absolute; TOP:60px; LEFT:250px;
BACKGROUND-COLOR:"skyblue"; WIDTH:400}
#layer3 {POSITION:absolute; TOP:200px; LEFT: 25px;
BACKGROUND-COLOR:"pink"}
-->
</STYLE>
```

Each layer name or identifier is proceeded by #, this is equivalent to an **ID** attribute in the **LAYER** tag. Note also that the set of layers are included within <!-- -->. Each layer has attributes to define coordinates of the layer and the layer's style.

NOLAYER tag

The **NOLAYER** tag works in exactly the same way as the **NOFRAME** tag. It allows us to examine whether the viewer browser enables the use of the **LAYER** tag or not. The following example shows the use of **NOLAYER** and viewing the file within Explorer.

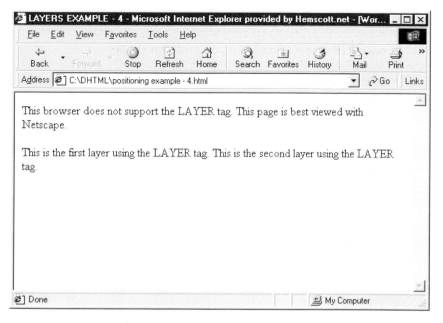

Fig 12.6 *Using the **NOLAYER** tag.*

Here is the code that I used earlier in figure 12.1 after including the **NOLAYER** tag:

```
<HTML>
<HEAD>
<TITLE>LAYERS EXAMPLE - 4</TITLE>
</HEAD>
<BODY>
<NOLAYER>
This browser does not support the LAYER tag.  This page is best viewed with
Netscape.
</NOLAYER>
<P>
<LAYER ID=layer1 TOP=20px LEFT=5px BGCOLOR= pink
width=600px>
This is the first layer using the LAYER tag.
</LAYER>
<LAYER ID=layer2 TOP=70px LEFT=200px BGCOLOR=yellow
width=200px>
This is the second layer using the LAYER tag.
</LAYER>
</BODY>
</HTML>
```

There are some more useful tricks you can use when using the **NOLAYER** tag. From the previous example and probably from your experience you know now that

LAYER tag works with Netscape only, at the same time you may have noticed that the CSS layers work better with Internet Explorer. By using the **NOLAYER** tag you can have both together and enable viewing of your page with both browsers. The following example shows this.

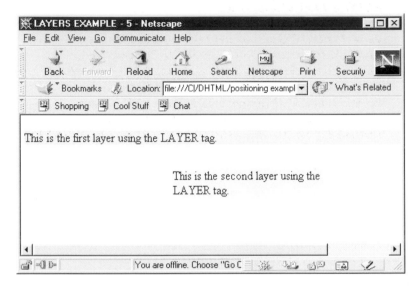

*Fig 12.7 Layers using the **LAYER** tag viewed by Netscape.*

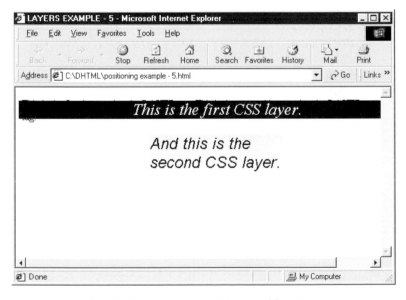

Fig 12.8 Layers using CSS viewed by IE.

Figures 12.7 and 12.8 both result from the following code:

```
<HTML>
<HEAD>
<TITLE>LAYERS EXAMPLE - 5</TITLE>
</HEAD>
<STYLE TYPE="text/css">
<!--
#layer1 {POSITION:absolute; TOP:20px; LEFT:5px;
TEXT-ALIGN:center; BACKGROUND-COLOR:black;
BORDER-WIDTH:10px; BORDER-COLOR:yellow; WIDTH:600px;
COLOR:white; FONT-SIZE:24; FONT-STYLE:italic}
#layer2 {POSITION:absolute;TOP:70px; LEFT:200px;
TEXT-ALIGN:left; BACKGROUND-COLOR:yellow;
BORDER-WIDTH:10pt; BORDER-COLOR:bluesky; WIDTH:200px;
COLOR:black; FONT-SIZE:24; FONT-STYLE:italic;
FONT-FAMILY:arial}
-->
</STYLE>
<BODY>
<NOLAYER>
<DIV ID=layer1>
This is the first CSS layer.
</DIV>
<DIV ID=layer2>
And this is the second CSS layer.
</DIV>
</NOLAYER>
<LAYER ID=layer1 TOP=20px LEFT=5px BGCOLOR=pink
WIDTH=600px>
This is the first layer using the LAYER tag.
</LAYER>
<LAYER ID=layer2 TOP=70px LEFT=200px BGCOLOR=yellow
WIDTH=200px>
This is the second layer using the LAYER tag.
</LAYER>
</BODY>
</HTML>
```

Note how the layers in CSS syntax and the **LAYER** tags are included together within the same HTML document. The CSS syntax layers are applied within the **NOLAYER** tag.

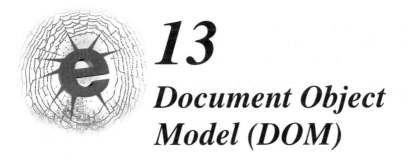

13
Document Object Model (DOM)

Introduction

The Document Object Model (DOM) is implemented in Microsoft and Netscape to allow the programming of each part of the document and its elements. DOM is based on the principles of object-oriented technology, however you do not need to be an expert to use DOM. In this chapter we shall learn the basics of DOM and how to use it, and we shall learn about a new tag that is closely related to the idea of an object model. We shall look at:

- What an object and its properties and methods mean.
- What events and event handling mean.
- An example of using DOM to open hyperlinks in new windows.
- The **OBJECT** tag.

Object, properties and methods

In the Document Object Model (DOM), everything we use in the web page is an object, and each object has properties and methods. Object refers to an instance of type, class or collection that is pre-defined. As an example, a document is a type where a web page is an object of that type.

A property refers to a feature or characteristic of an object usually appearing as attributes, such as the font colour.

A method refers to an action or an event that we can use to interact with the object, for example to change values of one of the object properties. The simplest way to illustrate this is to write a message in the object *document* using a method called *write*.

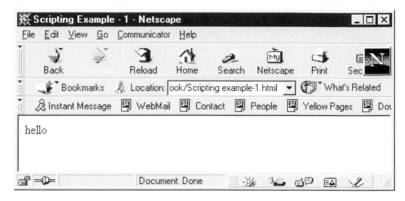

Fig 13.1 *Using DOM in Netscape.*

This example is achieved using the following code:

```
<HTML>
<TITLE>Scripting Example - 1</TITLE>
<BODY>
<SCRIPT LANGUAGE="JavaScript">
document.write ("hello")
</SCRIPT>
</BODY>
</HTML>
```

Notice how the '.' is used after the object name (**document**) to access the object method (**write**). Scripting and the **SCRIPT** tag are covered in more details in chapter 17. The examples in this chapter will help you to understand how DOM works and how you can use it to create dynamic web pages. They will also help you to understand JavaScript as they will include JavaScript syntax.

Events and event handling

Two of the most important aspects of DOM are events and event handling. Events are occurrences within the system that are usually triggered by the user. The clicking on a link or moving the mouse over an image are examples of events. These events can be used to invoke the execution of a script or code. Figure 13.2 shows an example of using the **onClick** event to set the *window's status bar* attribute to the text value of our choice.

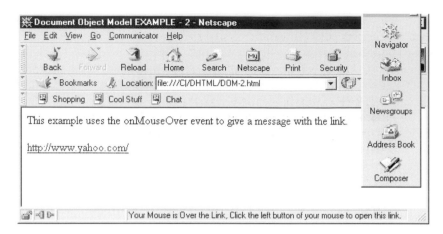

Fig 13.2 *Using DOM to provide a message on the Window's status bar.*

```
<HTML>
<TITLE>Document Object Model EXAMPLE - 2</TITLE>
<BODY>
This example uses the onMouseOver event to give a message with the link.
<P>
<A HREF="http://www.yahoo.com/"
onMouseOver="window.status='Your Mouse is Over the Link, Click the left
button of your mouse to open this link.'; return true">
http://www.yahoo.com/</A>
</BODY>
</HTML>
```

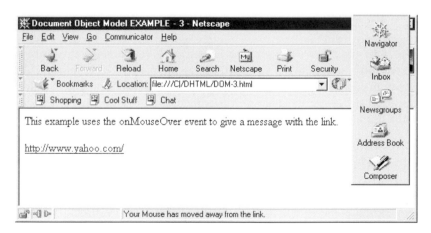

Fig 13.3 *Changing window status messages using DOM events.*

```
<HTML>
<TITLE>Document Object Model EXAMPLE - 3</TITLE>
<BODY>
This example uses the onMouseOver event to give a message with the link.
<P>
<A HREF="http://www.yahoo.com/"
onMouseOver="window.status='Your Mouse is Over the Link, Click the left
button of your mouse to open this link.'; return true"
onMouseOut="window.status='Your Mouse has moved away from the link.';
return true">
http://www.yahoo.com/</A>
</BODY>
</HTML>
```

Display in a new window

Have you ever wondered how web authors manage to force the browser to open a new window to display a web page or an image? All you need is a few lines of simple code added to your link:

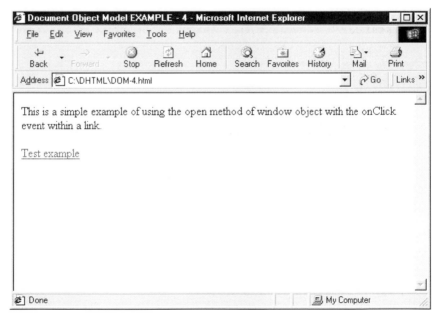

Fig 13.4 Using the Open method.

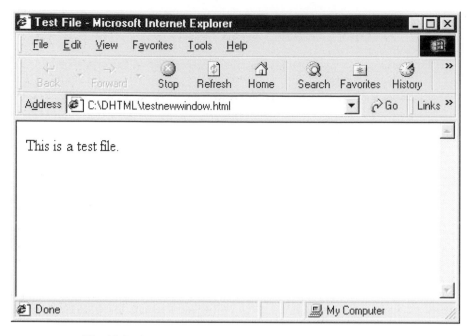

*Fig 13.5 The new window opened by the **open** method.*

The code that I have used to open a new window for my test file is:

```
<HTML>
<HEAD>
<TITLE>Document Object Model EXAMPLE - 4</TITLE>
</HEAD>
<BODY>
This is a simple example of using the open method of window object with the
onClick event within a link.
<P><A HREF="#" onClick='window.open("testnewwindow.html")'>
Test example</A>
</BODY>
</HTML>
```

Note that the use of the **open** method of the **window** object allows us to open the link in a new window. Notice also the **onClick** event which causes the **open** method to run.

```
<A HREF="#" onClick='window.open("testnewwindow.html")'>
Test example</A>
```

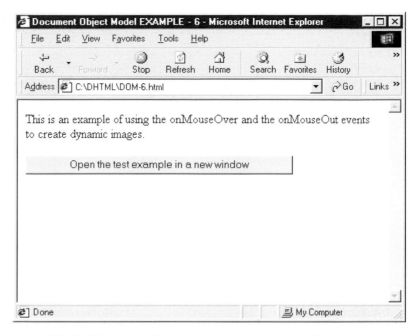

Fig 13.6 *Using the* **Open** *method with a command button.*

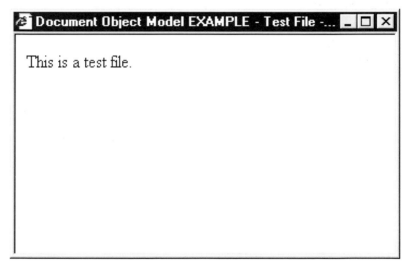

Fig 13.7 *The opened window without scroll bars.*

The code below produced the windows shown in figures 13.6 and 13.7. Notice the extra attributes that **open** method takes in this code which enabled me to control the dimensions of the display area.

```
<HTML>
<HEAD>
<TITLE>Document Object Model EXAMPLE - 6</TITLE>
</HEAD>
<BODY>
This is an example of using the onMouseOver and the onMouseOut events
to create dynamic images.
<FORM>
<INPUT TYPE="button" VALUE="Open the test example in a new
window" onClick='window.open("testnewwindow.html","testwindow",
"status=no, width=350, height=200")'>
</FORM>
</BODY>
</HTML>
```

OBJECT tag

I thought it might be more suitable to mention this tag in the DOM chapter than anywhere else. Considering multimedia components - video, audio and so on - we can think of them as objects. The same can apply to Java applets and data elements, etc. The **OBJECT** tag enables us to treat all data and multimedia objects in the same manner and include them in our web pages using one tag. It plays a very important role in data binding. However, **OBJECT** tag is a new extension to HTML.

Using DOM with JavaScript

DOM is not effective when used on its own. Using JavaScript with DOM gives much greater flexibility in creating dynamic and attractive web sites. Some understanding and usage of JavaScript is required, and some examples of using JavaScript can be seen in chapter 17.

Using DOM in CSS and layers

In chapters 11 and 12 we saw how we can define and use CSS and layers. However in all the examples we used the **ID** attribute to identify the style or layer when applying that style or layer to a part of our document. In this section we will look at how to define a style class and a layer class.

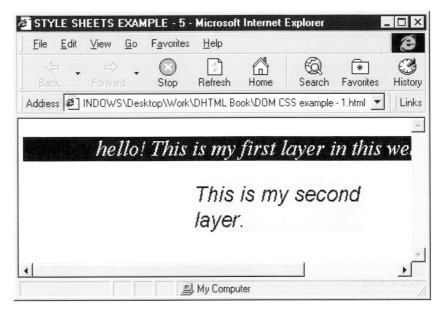

Fig 13.8 *Using layers defined as classes.*

Figure 13.8 is similar to figure 12.6 but it is coded in a different way:

```
<HTML>
<HEAD>
<TITLE>STYLE SHEETS EXAMPLE - 5</TITLE>
</HEAD>
<STYLE TYPE="text/css">
.layer1 {POSITION:absolute; TOP:20px; LEFT:5px; TEXT-ALIGN:
center; BACKGROUND-COLOR:black; border-width:10px; border-
color:yellow; width:600px; COLOR:white; FONT-SIZE: 24; FONT-
STYLE: ITALIC}
.layer2 {POSITION:absolute;TOP:70px; LEFT:200px;TEXT-ALIGN: left;
BACKGROUND-COLOR:yellow; border-width:10pt; border-color:bluesky;
width:200px; COLOR:black; FONT-SIZE: 24; FONT-STYLE: ITALIC;
FONT-FAMILY: arial}
</STYLE>
<body>
<DIV class=layer1>
hello! This is my first layer in this web page.
</DIV>
<DIV ID=layer class=layer2>
This is my second layer.
</DIV>
</body>
</HTML>
```

The first difference you may notice is the way layers are defined within the **STYLE** tag. In chapter 12 the layer name had '#' as a prefix, in this example it has '.'. Using '.' means that the layer is a class of style that can be used by many layer objects (child layers). As a result when these layers are used within the **DIV** tag they are referred to with a class attribute, while the section or child layer itself may have its own name using the **ID** attribute. This is the case with the second layer which we named *layer,* from the type *layer2*.

This concept of defining layers as objects is important in handling the layers and their content. It allows us to create and attach several effects to our layers.

14
Dynamic Positioning

Introduction

Dynamic positioning and dynamic contents (the latter is discussed in the next chapter) are important techniques used in DHTML. Cascading Style Sheets (CSS), layers and Document Object Model (DOM) are the tools that we use, and they function differently to achieve dynamic positioning, the reason being the incompatibility of browsers (for example the **LAYER** tag is best used with the Netscape browser while DOM and CSS are best used with Microsoft Explorer). It is important, therefore, to make sure that you are familiar with these tools or methods before you go any further.

We can achieve full dynamic positioning by using scripting with the concepts which will be presented in chapters 14 and 15. Scripting itself will be covered later on in chapter 17. In this chapter we shall concentrate on explaining the concept and looking at some examples of dynamic positioning:

- Relative and absolute positioning.
- Alternative forms of syntax for dynamic positioning.
- Using CSS layers and **LAYER** tags in dynamic positioning.

Relative vs. absolute positioning

Relative and absolute positioning are important principles in dynamic positioning. Layers are flexible frames that we can position and reposition as we wish. We may decide that a layer should stay in the same position on the screen regardless of what is happening to its surroundings. In this case the other elements and layers in the web page will either cover the layer or be covered by the layer whenever they use the same area. This may be our intention in some cases where we are using layers to hide each other creating a card-like system. However we may not want this to happen.

Relative positioning allows us to lay down our layers in relation to each other. As a result whenever a layer is extended or the window size is changed, the layers will move to fit next to each other. This could be seen as the simplest version of dynamic positioning.

To declare relatively positioned layers in CSS layers we have to use the **POSITION** attribute and declare the positioning explicitly that is relative. Alternatively we can use the **ILAYER** tag if we are writing for Netscape.

Alternative forms of syntax

To facilitate dynamic positioning in our web pages we have to use layers. That means we can use two forms of syntax: CSS layers and the **LAYER/ILAYER** tags. Netscape and Explorer handle layers in different ways, therefore we need to consider both ways of declaring layers and positioning them.

Note that even though they are different in syntax they are not different in principle. In fact dynamic positioning works in the same way whether CSS or **LAYER/ILAYER** tags are used. In both cases, however, some JavaScript is required. That should not prevent you from understanding the examples presented in this chapter. JavaScript is used to facilitate DOM and manipulate its objects.

We cover JavaScript basics for the general use of scripting in chapter 17. Using JavaScript utilises DHTML concepts and converts HTML to a full programming language. This allows us to create programs that run faster than the traditional Java applets or CGI scripts.

Using CSS in dynamic positioning

We are going to use the same example that we used in previous chapters to demonstrate the use of CSS in dynamic positioning. The difference here is that the second layer becomes a command button. We have to make this change as we need a means of initiating JavaScript. The alternative as we shall see in a later example is to use **<A>** tag.

Figure 14.1 shows the page as it was downloaded with the two layers.

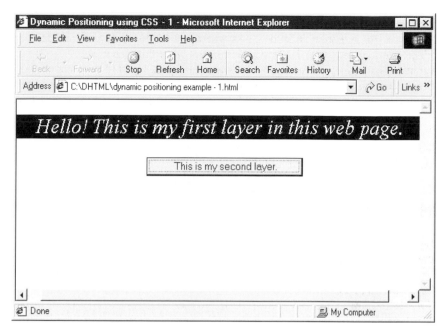

Fig. 14.1 *Loading the page in Explorer.*

Figure 14.2 shows the result of pressing on the second layer – the command button.

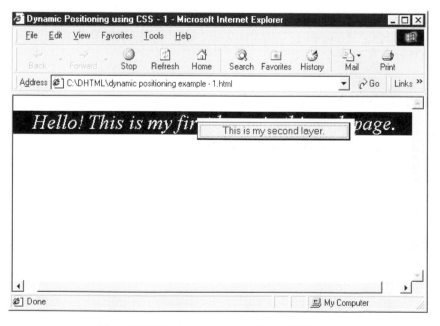

Fig. 14.2 *The button moves after clicking.*

Note how the second layer moved in response to the action event of clicking.   The HTML code that is needed for this dynamic positioning is:

```
<HTML>
<HEAD>
<TITLE>Dynamic Positioning using CSS - 1</TITLE>
</HEAD>
<SCRIPT>
function random(range)
{
    return (Math.round(((Math.random( ))*1000))%range)+1;
}
function movelayer( )
{
    document.all['mylayer2'].style.left=random(300);
    document.all['mylayer2'].style.top=random(300);
}
</SCRIPT>
<STYLE TYPE="text/css">
.layer1 {POSITION:absolute; TOP:20px; LEFT:5px; TEXT-
ALIGN:center; BACKGROUND-COLOR:black; BORDER-WIDTH:10px;
BORDER-COLOR:yellow; WIDTH:600px; COLOR:white; FONT-
SIZE:20pt; FONT-STYLE:italic}
.layer2 {POSITION:absolute;TOP:70px; LEFT:200px; TEXT-ALIGN: left;
BACKGROUND-COLOR:yellow; BORDER-WIDTH:10pt; BORDER-
COLOR:bluesky; WIDTH:200px; COLOR:black; FONT-SIZE: 20pt;
FONT-STYLE:italic; FONT-FAMILY:arial}
</STYLE>
<BODY>
<DIV CLASS=layer1>
hello! This is my first layer in this web page.
</DIV>
<DIV ID=mylayer2 CLASS=layer2>
<FORM>
<INPUT TYPE=button VALUE="This is my second layer."
ONCLICK="movelayer()">
</FORM>
</DIV>
</BODY>
</HTML>
```

Notice the scripting section where we used JavaScript to achieve the actual movement.

```
<SCRIPT>
function random(range)
{
```

```
    return (Math.round(((Math.random())*1000))%range)+1;
}
function movelayer()
{
    document.all['mylayer2'].style.left=random(300);
    document.all['mylayer2'].style.top=random(300);
}
</SCRIPT>
```

Scripting in general and JavaScript in particular will be covered in more detail in chapter 17. However let us study this area of JavaScript and what it does. There are two functions: the *random* function gives us a random number while the *movelayer* function moves the selected layer – in this case *mylayer2* – to a random position given by *random* function. The *movelayer* function does this by using DOM to reassign the values of the *left* and *top* attributes of the *style* of the *layer* object to the random number that is generated by *random* function. This is generally how dynamic positioning is done. The values of the attributes can be random values as in this example or pre-determined values.

Let us look now at the definition of the second layer.

```
<DIV ID=mylayer2 CLASS=layer2>
<FORM>
<INPUT TYPE=button VALUE="This is my second layer."
onClick="movelayer( )">
</FORM>
</DIV>
```

Note in this definition the use of the **FORM** tag includes the button. Also note the use of the DOM event **onClick** in the **INPUT** tag to invoke the *movelayer* function. This is generally how JavaScript functions are invoked to create an interactive response.

Using the LAYER/ILAYER tags in dynamic positioning

Dynamic positioning is done using the **LAYER/ILAYER** tags in a similar manner to the CSS layers. The **LAYER/ILAYER** tags are used in the same way as the **DIV** tag, however there is no need to define the style before using the **LAYER/ILAYER** tags. Therefore we will not use the **STYLE** tag, instead the definition of the style will be included within the **LAYER/ILAYER** tags. The drawback of this technique appears in modifying our DHTML documents as we have to search for the **LAYER/ILAYER** tags to change the style.

Figure 14.3 shows the same page in Netscape created using the **LAYER** tag.

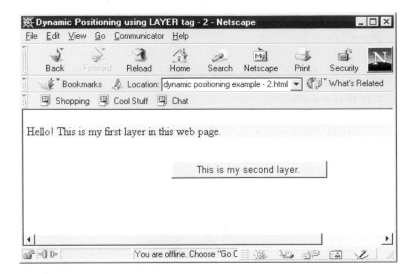

Fig. 14.3 *Using the **LAYER/ILAYER** tags in Netscape.*

Figure 14.4 shows the page after using the JavaScript function *movelayer*.

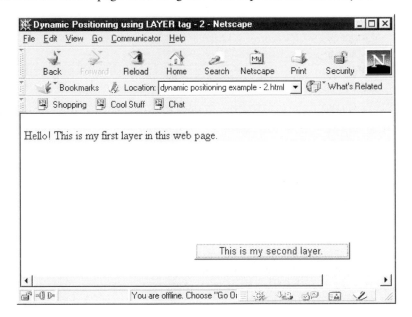

Fig. 14.4 *The button moves in response to the **onClick** event.*

The HTML code is almost the same as the previous example:

```
<HTML>
<HEAD>
<TITLE>Dynamic Positioning using LAYER tag - 2</TITLE>
</HEAD>
```

```
<SCRIPT>
function random(range)
{
    return (Math.round(((Math.random())*1000))%range)+1;
}
function movelayer()
{
    document.layers['mylayer2'].left=random(300);
    document.layers['mylayer2'].top=random(300);
}
</SCRIPT>
<BODY>
<LAYER ID=mylayer1 TOP=20px LEFT=5px BGCOLOR=pink
WIDTH=600px>
Hello! This is my first layer in this web page.
</LAYER>
<LAYER ID=mylayer2 TOP=70px LEFT=200px BGCOLOR=yellow
WIDTH=200px>
<FORM>
<INPUT TYPE=button VALUE="This is my second layer."
ONCLICK="movelayer()">
</FORM>
</LAYER>
</BODY>
</HTML>
```

The first difference you may notice is in the DOM sentences in JavaScript function *movelayer*.

```
function movelayer()
{
    document.layers['mylayer2'].left=random(300);
    document.layers['mylayer2'].top=random(300);
}
```

DOM as it is implemented in Netscape recognises the layers that are defined by the **LAYER/ILAYER** tags as objects. As a result, the DOM sentences when they are used to handle **LAYER** tags contain explicit reference to layers as a class of objects. This allows better object-oriented handling of layers. As a result we can set directly the **LEFT** and **TOP** attributes of the layer object.

Try to catch the ship

This is a trick you can add to your site for fun. Figure 14.5 shows an image of a ship and a prompt asks the viewer to catch the ship.

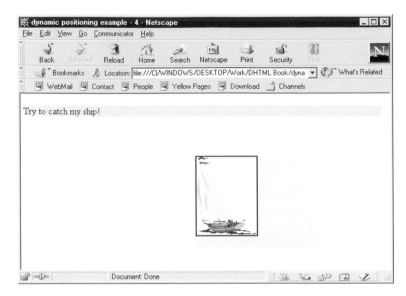

Fig. 14.5 *Page downloads with the ship in the middle.*

What the viewer does not know is that the ship is supported by dynamic positioning script that makes it move to a new random position every time the mouse moves over it.

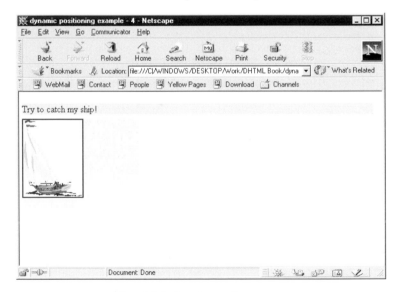

Fig. 14.6 *The ship sails away.*

The code you need to create this application is similar to the code we used earlier in this chapter:

```
<HTML>
<HEAD>
```

```
<TITLE>dynamic positioning example - 4</TITLE>
</HEAD>
<SCRIPT>
function random(range)
{
    return (Math.round(((Math.random( ))*1000))%range)+1;

}
function movelayer()

{
    document.layers['mylayer2'].left=random(300);
    document.layers['mylayer2'].top=random(300);
}
</SCRIPT>
<BODY>
<LAYER ID=mylayer1 TOP=20px LEFT=5px BGCOLOR=pink
width=600px>
Try to catch my ship!
</LAYER>
<LAYER ID=mylayer2 TOP=70px LEFT=200px BGCOLOR=yellow
width=200px>
<A HREF="#" onMouseOver="movelayer()">
<P><IMG Name="ship" SRC="Image1.gif" WIDTH=100
HEIGHT=130></P>
</LAYER>
</BODY>
</HTML>
```

Note here there are two things different from previous examples. First, the use of
<A> tag to invoke the JavaScript. Second, the use of the **onMouseOver** event instead
of the **onClick** event. To know what other events are available you need to download
the DOM documentation of Netscape and Explorer from the Internet.

15
Dynamic Contents

Introduction

Dynamic content technology relies on a similar concept to dynamic positioning. But instead of changing the position in a dynamic way, the page contents are changed dynamically. The changes can affect any of the page objects including font, colour, text and so on.

In this chapter we will be looking at this technology and how we can use it to enhance our web pages. You will learn how to:

- Use DOM to change the contents dynamically.
- Show different images when the mouse passes over the image.
- Use simple JavaScript code to change contents dynamically.

Dynamic images using DOM

The best way to show how to create a page with dynamic content is to use an example. The one we are going to look at allows you to show different images as the user passes the mouse over the current image. To do so we are going to use the event **onMouseOver**.

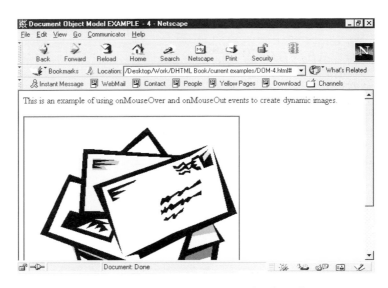

Fig 15.1 *First image that appears when loading the page.*

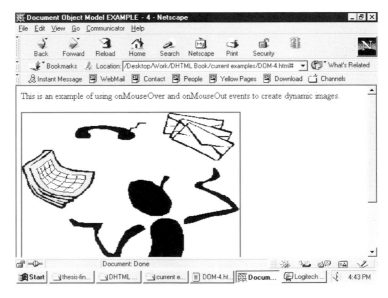

Fig 15.2 *Image that is shown when the mouse is over the image in figure 15.1.*

The code that you need to create dynamic images using DOM, shown below, does not contain any JavaScript functions:

```
<HTML>
<TITLE> Document Object Model EXAMPLE - 4</TITLE>
<BODY>
This is an example of using onMouseOver and onMouseOut events to create
```

dynamic images.

```
<P><A HREF="#" onMouseOver="lettersimage.src='image4.gif'; return
true;" onMouseOut="lettersimage.src='image5.gif'; return true;">
<IMG SRC="Image5.gif" NAME=lettersimage>
</A>
</BODY>
</HTML>
```

Before you try this code you need to get two images. I called mine *image4.gif* and *image5.gif* but you can use any names for your images. It is advisable to use meaningful names. Once you have prepared your images you can use the above code with your images' names. Figure 15.1 shows the image which is displayed first, while figure 15.2 shows the image displayed when the mouse is moved over it.

<IMG SRC="Image5.gif" NAME=lettersimage>

To change the images you have to use the **NAME** attribute in the **IMG** tag to identify your object – the image – then you use that name with the attribute **SRC**, which is associated with image objects, to change the image, as we can see from this code extract:

<A HREF="#" onMouseOver="lettersimage.src='image4.gif'; return true;"
onMouseOut="lettersimage.src='image5.gif'; return true;">

There are three important points to note:

- The image object is referred to by the image name *lettersimage* which has the attribute **SRC** that is used to change the image.
- The use of the scope identifier '.' after the name *lettersimage* to access the attribute **SRC**.
- The use of the **onMouseOver** event to apply the changes as a result of this event occurrence.

By using image links you can change the look of a link every time the viewer passes his/her mouse over it. The image could be a picture or text which is stored in an image format. Also the change does not need to be a completely new image; it could just be a change, for example, in the background colour of the image link.

16
Managing a Dynamic Site

Introduction

If you have read all of the earlier chapters of this book you will have learned all the basic skills needed to produce a dynamic web site. In this chapter we are going to look at managing our dynamic web sites, my aim being to bring together the skills you have learnt so far. We shall look at:

- Design issues.
- Debugging.
- Publishing a dynamic site.
- Managing a dynamic site including managing contents.

Design issues

We have already looked at some design issues in chapter 9. In this section we are going to focus on design in general in the light of the techniques we have learnt so far. The design process has been broken down into the stages that I usually use when I design and build a web site. However, feel free to merge stages, split them or even change their order as you think appropriate.

The first stage is to make decisions on some basic design issues. For example, are you going to use frames or layers? How many pages do you need? What are the links between these pages? Do you need to use forms? At this stage I usually use a form of storyboarding to tell the story of the site. In other words, I draw a rough plan of different web pages in the site and the links between these pages.

Once I have my list of pages I start to think about their contents. What will each page present and how much information will be covered. At this stage you may find yourself altering the number of pages. Too little information in a web page is as bad as too much. If we have too little information we will end up with too many pages and too many links. This means that users may have to go through numerous links before getting to what they want. On the other hand if there is too much in a web page, it will be difficult to read. As a general rule a web page should have as much information as can be displayed in a single screen.

Once the number of pages and their contents are clear we can start thinking about tools. Are we going to write the HTML tags ourselves or use authoring tools? Do we need photo and graphics editors? Are we going to use sound, video and animations? It is a good idea to know your resources before you start actually designing the web site and deciding what will be included and where.

The final stage is to decide on what techniques we are going to use. Are we going to use frames or layers? Are there any forms and what are they for? Are we going to use JavaScript, CSS or the LAYER tag? The issues will affect how we build the site and what contents we put on the pages. In other words, how are we going to present our layout and what are the techniques that will enable us to do this? It may be a good idea if you refer to layout design in chapter 9.

Debugging a DHTML site

Once you have built your site you have to make sure it works. When we say a site is working we mean that the appearance of the site is similar to what we intended with our design and that all the links and scripts are correct. The process of checking the site and fixing any errors is called debugging.

The easiest way to debug your site is by running it using a Web browser. This shows how it looks and we can spot any unsuitable design decisions – for example inappropriate font size – as well as any errors in using HTML tags and scripting.

As for HTML tags, the most common error is to forget to close the tag or quotation mark of the tag attributes values. If there is an error in an HTML tag, the browser may not read the tag at all and the effects expected from the tag will not be shown on the page.

The difficult part is debugging the scripts that we may have included in our web pages. While there are tools to help us debug JavaScript such as the Microsoft debugging tools in IE, we may need to develop our own techniques to debug our CSS and layers. Remember that we may have saved our CSS and layers scripts in separate files, which means if the style we see on the screen is not what we intended then the error may be in one of the external CSS files. The first step is to identify which style is not working properly and try to associate that with one of the CSS files. It is a good idea to label your external CSS so you know which style is saved in which file. Once the file is identified then try to identify the style that is not working within the file and go through it slowly. You may not have closed one of the quotation marks or have missed a semicolon. Also you may have used an attribute that is not supported by the browser you are using.

It is a good idea to view your web page with more than one browser. I would suggest using both Netscape and Microsoft IE. If you are creating web pages on a professional level then checking these web pages appear correctly in a variety of used browsers will be useful. (Even though Netscape and IE are the most used browsers, there are still people who are using other browsers.)

Publishing a site

Once you have designed and built your site, it is time to publish your creative product. Publishing your site includes installing it on the server and then making sure that other users will visit this site.

There is often a directory created for you on the Internet Service Provider (ISP) server and in that directory you can install your web site with any directories you may need. When you install your site on the server make sure that all the components of that site are included in your designated directory including any code files – for example external style sheets that your site uses. Try to make the links between your web pages relatively addressed links instead of fixed addressed links so that moving the site from your hard disk to the server does not affect your site.

When it comes to advertising your web site there are different ways of doing this. The first is to submit your site to a search engine. You can do this on the web as many search engines provide a form that allows you to submit your web site address and some details about yourself and your web site. Netscape search engine comes to mind as an example. An alternative way is to make it noticeable to other search engines as it may not be possible to submit your web site address to all search engines on the web. You can do that by using the **META** tag within the **HEAD** section of your web page. The general format of the **META** tag is the following:

<META NAME="Date" CONTENT="10/11/96">

The **NAME** attribute usually takes a keyword that describes what this tag is about, while the **CONTENT** tag contains the actual value of the tag. As an example, you can use *Description* keyword as a value of the **NAME** attribute instead of *Date* in the above code to describe your web page, and your description becomes the value of **CONTENT** tag instead of *10/11/96*. In the same way you can use *Keywords* keyword in the **META** tag to list keywords related to your web page. You can include **META** tags to each of your web pages or just the main web page in your site, but usually there are at least two **META** tags: *Description* and *Keywords*.

<META HTTP-EQUIV="Description" NAME="Description"
CONTENT="Here comes your description of your web page">
<META HTTP-EQUIV="Keywords" NAME="Keywords"
CONTENT="list of keywords for your web page, separat these keywords
with commas">

The **HTTP-EQUIV** attribute takes the same keywords that the **NAME** attribute takes. Adding the **META** tag to each web page will increase the chances of viewers looking at your web page, and will allow you to add web pages that may have different content themes which is very likely to happen in personal sites.

The second way is to submit it to a directory such as Link Exchange. Most of these directories are free, the main principle being that you advertise on their members web pages in return for having an advertisement on your web page. They usually give you a code to add to a web page within your site.

News groups are alternative ways to publicise your site. You can include your site address with some details and post a message to the news group of your choice. Make sure that you post your web site address to relevant news groups. (If your site has music as its main theme, then posting its address to news groups that are concerned with networks or the share market may irritate them.)

Managing a DHTML site

We can all find it annoying to view out of date web sites. In this section I will be giving some tips on how to manage both the content and the look of your web site. First of all, however, you have to establish a local working directory because editing a web page that resides on the server will prevent other users from viewing it. Working in a workshop-like directory will reduce the time during which the site is off-line. For more major web site repairs and maintenance, it is a good idea to create a simple web page to replace the web site or web pages that are taken off-line with a simple message to tell viewers what is happening.

When you manage your site contents you have to plan carefully. First you should decide which parts of your site are going to be updated or changed. Make a list of the web pages which the changes will affect, and the parts within these web pages which will be affected. Once this is done, try to find any contradiction or inter-relationship between the new changes and the rest of your web site contents, especially if you are changing links or adding whole new pages.

When deciding on the appearance of your site you have to rely very much on what is common practice in the Internet community. I have learned a lot just from looking at existing sites and the code that is written behind those sites. Watch for aspects of web page design already covered in chapters 5 and 9, and try to determine which background is used, how the front elements are laid out, what font colours are used, why they used these colours and what are the effects of the design. You often learn more from badly designed sites than from good ones. When you think the site is badly designed try to figure out the reason and avoid it in your own design.

Once you have done your research and decided it is time to change the look of your site, make a list of what is going to be changed, where the changes will take place and the effects of these changes on other elements of the web page. You may also like to make a list of different techniques which you can use to make these changes more effective. In all your design decisions, make sure that there is a design standard used in all of the web pages in your site or a general design context to make viewers feel that they are still in the same site.

17
Scripting

Introduction

We have experienced some scripting in previous chapters. In this chapter we shall explore scripting which is included within an HTML document, and in Common Gate Interface (CGI) scripting. The main principle behind embedded scripting within an HTML document is to control the web page from the client-side rather than from the server, as is the case with CGI scripting. Controlling web pages from the client-side is becoming common practice and may hold the key to more successful dynamic sites. The rest of this chapter covers JavaScript basics since JavaScript is the most frequently used scripting language within HTML documents.

We are going to look at an overview of:

- The SCRIPT tag.
- The APPLET tag.
- JScript, VBScript and Perl script.
- CGI scripting.
- JavaScript basics.
- JavaScript functions.

SCRIPT tag

The **SCRIPT** tag enables us to include scripts within an HTML document. We have already seen an example in chapter 13. It usually shares the **HEAD** section of the document with the **TITLE** and **META** tags. The **LANGUAGE** attribute defines the type of the scripting language we are using. If it is omitted the **SCRIPT** tag will assume that JavaScript is used. We will see more of the **SCRIPT** tag later in this chapter when we look at the basics of JavaScript.

APPLET tag

It is worth mentioning another tag that is associated with scripting the **APPLET** tag which allows us to include Java applets in our HTML documents. Java applets are usually used to create animation and visual effects and to handle data. The **APPLET** tag syntax is simply:

> *<APPLET CODE= "JavaApplet.class" WIDTH=100 HEIGHT=50>*
> *</APPLET>*

   This is the simple version of the **APPLET** tag. However there are other tags that may appear within the **APPLET** tag, such as the **PARAM** tag. However the **OBJECT** tag is becoming the standard tag for inserting any objects in documents including programs and applets, and hence it replaces the **APPLET** tag in HTML 4.0.

JavaScript and JScript

It is very easy to confuse JavaScript and JScript, even though both of them use similar syntax to the Java programming language. JavaScript was developed to work on the client-side and is the most commonly used scripting language in DHTML. JScript on the other hand is a server-side scripting language which you may never have to use.

VBScript

VBScript is a new alternative to JavaScript based on Visual Basic language, and as you may expect, is a Microsoft invention. It does not work on all browsers and in fact you need a plug-in to use VBScript even with Microsoft Internet Explorer. You can download this plug-in from the Microsoft site. VBScript is becoming more popular as more people are using Visual Basic.

Perl script

Perl script is based on the Perl language in the same way that JavaScript is based on Java. Perl is a programming language which belongs to the open software category similar in that sense to Linux. It is associated in particular with programming for the Internet, in particular CGI scripting, and is a simpler version of the language used within HTML. Perl script, however, needs a plug-in to enable the browser to interpret it as it is not supported by most browsers. You can find this plug-in on the Microsoft and

Netscape sites. Because Perl is an open software there are many developments coming from different sources. If you are planning to use Perl and Perl script – and it might be advisable to do so if you are interested in CGI scripting – it would pay to join a news group or discussion group for this language. These groups are very active and informative.

CGI scripting

Common Gate Interface or CGI scripting enables server-side programming and allows the server to receive and send data. Even though it is called scripting it can be done in any language such as Fortran, C++, Java, VB and so on. In fact CGI scripting is not a language or scripting as such, instead it is a framework for sending and receiving messages. The messages that are received and sent have headers with pre-defined sub-strings and they include field names. In other words the received data is not formatted for use in databases and the retrieved data from the database cannot be formatted to deliver through HTTP protocol to the browser.

Nowadays more tools are available to replace the use of CGI scripting. Cold Fusion is one of them. You can also use data binding which is described in the next chapter. Visual Basic and Access also provide some tools to convert data into a web suitable form, and big database management systems have become involved in this area. ORACLE, for example, released its own database web server component to enable the use of the ORACLE database system with Internet technology. However, CGI scripting is still important when a complex system with lots of information traffic is required.

Basics of JavaScript

In this section we shall be looking at the basics of JavaScript. We have seen some examples of JavaScript in earlier chapters when we discussed event handling in DOM and in dynamic contents. Understanding objects, methods and event handling is important when you work with JavaScript. You may like to refer to chapter 13 to review objects and event handling before you read further.

The first aspect of JavaScript that we are going to look at is the provision of some output to the user. Here is an example of how to use the message box or give an alert message using JavaScript in your DHTML code.

Fig 17.1 *Message window using the **alert** method.*

The code you need to do this is straightforward:

```
<HTML>
<HEAD>
<TITLE>Scripting Example - 2</TITLE>
</HEAD>
<BODY>
<SCRIPT LANGUAGE="JavaScript">
document.write ("<H2> This example shows how to use some methods of
document and window objects")
window.alert("Hello, this is an alert message.")
</SCRIPT>
</BODY>
</HTML>
```

Note the use of two methods of the object **document**:**write** – which we saw in chapter 13 – and the **alert**. While the **write** method writes to the document the **alert** method shows a message box. Note also that the **SCRIPT** tag is included within the **BODY** tag in this example this is because the script uses a pre-defined method of a Document Object Model (DOM). Later in this chapter we shall see the use of the **SCRIPT** tag within the **HEAD** section of the document.

Now we shall look at how you can accept input from the user as well as give an output through a message box. To accept input you can use the input box as shown in figure 17.2.

Fig 17.2 *Alert message.*

The code you need to take the user name and display it on the web page is:

```
<HTML>
<HEAD>
<TITLE>Scripting Example - 3</TITLE>
</HEAD>
<BODY>
<SCRIPT LANGUAGE="JavaScript">
document.write ("<H2> This example shows how to use some methods of
document and window objects.</H2>")
document.write("<CENTER><H3>")
document.write(window.prompt("Enter your name:", ""))
document.write("</CENTER></H3>")
```

```
</SCRIPT>
</BODY>
</HTML>
```

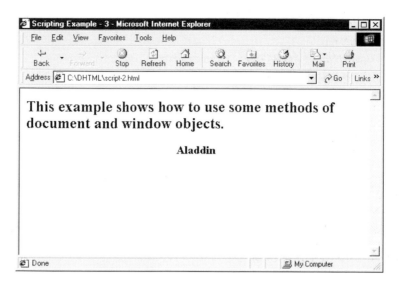

*Fig 17.3 Writing viewer name taken from an **alert** message box.*

Note the use of the **prompt** method which is a method of **window** object. Also notice the use of this method within the **write** method of the **document** object and the use of HTML tags within the **write** method.

It is interesting if you can welcome your web site viewer by name, as I did in figure 17.4 using a combination of the **prompt** method with the **write** method.

Fig 17.4 Welcoming the viewer by name.

The code I have used is a slightly modified version of the previous example:

```
<HTML>
<HEAD>
<TITLE>Scripting Example - 4</TITLE>
</HEAD>
<BODY>
<SCRIPT LANGUAGE="JavaScript">
document.write ("<CENTER><H1>Welcome to my web
site</H1></CENTER>")
document.write("<CENTER><ITALIC><H3> Dear ")
document.write(window.prompt("Enter your name:", ""))
document.write("</CENTER></ITALIC></H3>")
</SCRIPT>
</BODY>
</HTML>
```

There is no limit to what you can do with the few lines of JavaScript you have learned already. From the above code you may wonder if we can use variables to hold the information given back to us by the **window.prompt**? Here is an example which shows how easy it is to use variables in JavaScript. They do not need to be declared, you just use them when you need them.

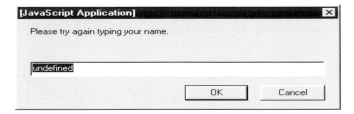

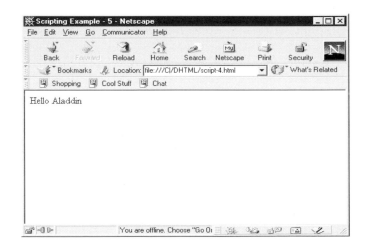

*Fig 17.5 Make sure that the user has entered his name by using the **while** loop.*

The example also shows other facilities provided by JavaScript such as the **while** loop. The following code checks whether the user has entered his name or not:

```
<HTML>
<HEAD>
<TITLE>Scripting Example - 5</TITLE>
</HEAD>
<BODY>
<SCRIPT LANGUAGE="JavaScript">
myname=""
myname=prompt("Enter your name here, please.", myname)
while (myname == "" || myname=="undefined")
{
    myname=prompt("Please try again typing your name.")
}
document.write("Hello "+myname)
</SCRIPT>
</BODY>
</HTML>
```

We need to look at the use of the variable *myname*. First we give it null value and we call this initialising the variable:

```
myname=""
```

Then we use the variable within the **prompt** method to receive the user's input into that variable:

```
myname=prompt("Enter your name here, please.", myname)
```

Note that if the user does not enter a name, our variable *myname* will have the value null. If that happens we have to ask the user again to enter a name. We can do this by using a **while** loop:

```
while (myname == "" || myname=="undefined")
{
    myname=prompt("Please try again typing your name")
}
```

Note the **while** keyword which is followed by a condition which controls the loop. As long as the condition is true the loop will keep going around executing the statements that are included within {}. In this example the loop will keep asking the user for a name as long as he does not enter a name. In the next example, shown in figure 17.6, I have used a different loop called the **for** loop.

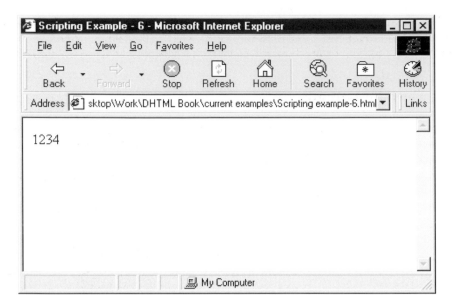

Fig 17.6 *Using the for loop.*

The code that you need for the **for** loop is:

```
<HTML>
<HEAD>
<TITLE>Scripting Example - 6</TITLE>
</HEAD>
<BODY>
<SCRIPT LANGUAGE="JavaScript">
for (counter=1; (counter<5); counter++)
{
document.write(counter)
}
</SCRIPT>
</BODY>
</HTML>
```

This type of loop is used when we want a specific number of repetitions. In other words the statements between {} will be executed the number of times equal to the number we specify.

```
for (counter=1; (counter<5); counter++)
{
document.write(counter)
}
```

Notice that our loop will run as long as the counter is less than 5. Since we have initialised the counter to 1, that means the loop will run four times. Figure 17.6 shows the result of this loop by numbers printed on the document using the **write** method.

JavaScript functions

If you have any experience with programming this section will seem familiar. However, if you do not there is no need to worry. A function is a simple concept. Usually it just involves using the same code over and over again. There is the choice between re-writing that code wherever it is needed or using a function to hold that block of code. By giving that function a name you can use that name wherever the code is required instead of repeating the same code again. Using the function name is called calling the function.

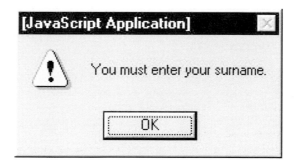

Fig 17.7 *Form with data-entry JavaScript checker.*

This simple booking form has a code to make sure that the user enters his surname:

```
<HTML>
<HEAD>
<TITLE>Scripting Example - 1</TITLE>
<SCRIPT LANGUAGE="JavaScript">
function validate()
```

```
{
if (document.myform.surname.value == "")
    {
    alert("You must enter your surname.");
    return;
    }
document.myform.submit();
}
</SCRIPT>
</HEAD>
<BODY>
<FORM NAME="myform">
<H1>Booking Form</H1>
First Name:
<INPUT NAME="firstname"><P>
Surname:
<INPUT NAME="surname"><P>
<INPUT TYPE="button" VALUE="Book now" onClick="validate()">
</FORM>
</BODY>
</HTML>
```

The function we have written validates the entry of the surname. This forces the user to enter his surname in the form. In using functions we have to consider two parts, the function code and the function call.

The function code starts with **function** keyword:

```
<SCRIPT LANGUAGE="JavaScript">
function validate( )
{
if (document.myform.surname.value == "")
    {
    alert("You must enter your surname.");
    return;
    }
document.myform.submit();
}
</SCRIPT>
```

The function code is included in the **SCRIPT** tag, which is usually placed in the **HEAD** section of the document. It is always the case when we are building our own functions.

Calling the function executes the functions statements. Without calling the function, the code will never be run. We call the function by using its name, a good reason to have a memorable and meaningful function name:

```
<INPUT TYPE="button" VALUE="Book now" onClick="validate( )">
```

In our example, we use the **onClick** event to invoke the function. Once the user clicks on the button *Book now,* the function *validate* will be called to check the form entry prior to sending it. This time we only checked the surname field, but, nothing prevents us from checking other fields at the same time. Figure 17.8 shows a message we can give before submission to give the user the chance to change their minds if there are any errors we did not detect.

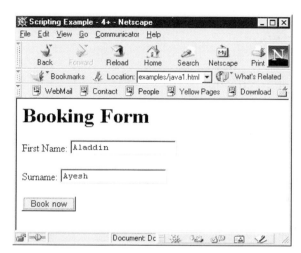

***Fig 17.8** JavaScript **alert** before submission of the details.*

The HTML and JavaScript code used to produce figure 17.8 is shown below:

```
<HTML>
<HEAD>
<TITLE>Scripting Example - 4+</TITLE>
<SCRIPT LANGUAGE="JavaScript">
function validate()
{
if (document.myform.firstname.value == "")
    {
    alert("You must enter your first name.");
```

```
        return;
        }
else if (document.myform.surname.value == "")
        {
        alert("You must enter your surname.");
        return;
        }
submitnow=confirm ("Do you want to submit now?")
if (submitnow)
{
        document.myform.submit();
}
else
{
        return
}
}
</SCRIPT>
</HEAD>
<BODY>
<FORM NAME="myform">
<H1>Booking Form</H1>
First Name:
<INPUT NAME="firstname"><P>
Surname:
<INPUT NAME="surname"><P>
<INPUT TYPE="button" VALUE="Book now" onClick="validate()">
</FORM>
</BODY>
</HTML>
```

Let us extract the function validate and look at it closely:

```
function validate()
{
if (document.myform.firstname.value == "")
        {
        alert("You must enter your first name.");
        return;
        }
else if (document.myform.surname.value == "")
        {
        alert("You must enter your surname.");
        return;
        }
sumbitnow=confirm ("Do you want to submit now?")
if (submitnow)
```

```
{
    document.myform.submit();
}
else
{
    return
}
}
```

Note the use of conditional statements starting with **if** or **else if**. These statements allow different statements to be executed. The first **if** checks that the first name has been entered. The first **else if** checks that the surname has been entered. This **else if** will not be used unless the first name has already been entered. If the first name and surname have been entered then we move to the second **else if** clause which asks for final confirmation from the user before sending the form. If the user confirms, then the form will be sent, otherwise the last *else* will be executed and the *return* statement will take us back to the HTML code without change.

Using JavaScript

JavaScript is a scripting language. That means we can use it to build complete programs within an HTML document. It is impossible for me to cover all the aspects of JavaScript programming here but you can further develop your skills using the basics you have learned in this chapter.

18
What is Next?

Introduction

There are two topics of DHTML technology that have not been covered yet:

- Data binding.
- Downloadable fonts.

DHTML is a new technology that is evolving on a daily basis. In this chapter we shall briefly cover these two topics. In addition, I shall be suggesting how you can progress from here.

Data binding

Data binding is one of the most important and complicated features of DHTML. If you remember from our early chapters on DHTML, the objective of DHTML is to reduce the need for server-based processes, so that we can do more client-based web page presentation work. Data binding is a technique to enforce this principle. By using data binding we can bind our web pages to a data source, which then retrieves the data at the load time but manipulates that data on the client-side without the need to make any reference to the server. This provides us with the means to access and process data very quickly and make the presentation of our web pages more informative and user specific.

This aspect of DHTML is very important to know and master if your final goal is in the e-commerce field. However, due to the difficult nature of this topic, I shall be covering the basics of data binding in this section leaving the door open for further study.

Data binding relies on defining Data Source Objects (DSO). By using DSOs we can define the following features of how the web page and the data are bound together:

- The transport mechanism that is going to be used in the case of transporting data, in other words the protocol used for information flow, for example HTTP.
- The mechanism that is used for data specification, for example SQL.
- The functions that may be used for manipulating data. Some of the usual examples would be the sorting and filtering of data.
- How the updating data mechanism is supported.
- Finally, DSOs provide an object model for scripting which may be influenced by the DSO that is used.

Currently there are three ways of getting and using DSOs:

- Tabular Data Control.
- JDBC Data Provider.
- Microsoft Remote Data Services.

Tabular Data Control

The Tabular Data Control (TDC) is so called because it is limited to reading and displaying data in tabular format. TDC does not provide us with data updating facilities but we are still able to sort and filter our data. The good thing about TDC is the fact that it is installed automatically when we install Internet Explorer version 4 or above.

You have to keep the text file of TDC on the same host as the page that is containing the TDC instance. The first line of the text file is usually the field names which you can use when you create the HTML template. You can also specify the fields' data type for more efficient sorting and filtering.

JDBC Data Provider

Java DataBase Connector (JDBC) Data Provider is a Java applet that is available through the Microsoft web site. This applet allows us to link our web page to any ODBC-compatible data source. ODBC or Object DataBase Connectivity is becoming a standard way of handling objects in databases.

The main drawback of the JDBC Data Provider is that the client-side must have the ODBC data source specified in the applet's properties. This may not cause much of a problem if you are controlling the network - in other words if the users of your web page are on a local network or are direct clients for whom you are installing all required parts of their system. However, for distant global viewers it may prove to be difficult.

The JDBC Data Provider is similar to TDC in its capabilities. However one of the advantages of JDBC is that the source code is available for Java programmers to develop it further to their needs. Additionally we can use database files, such as MS Access, with JDBC instead of text files as is the case with TDC.

Microsoft Remote Data Services

By now you may be wondering how can we update database files through the use of DSOs. So far we can retrieve the data and present it, but how do we receive data and update the relevant fields? If you are interested in doing so then you may need to consider Microsoft Remote Data Services (RDS) or Advanced Data Connector (the two terms refer to the same thing). RDS provides us with the capability of updating the data in our databases. In addition it provides us with the following capabilities:

- We can create what is known as three-tiered applications using data-bound HTML.
- We can use Microsoft ODBC and OLE DB to provide a consistent front-end for the back-end data source regardless of its format.
- The ODBC data source only needs to reside on the server-side. This makes the application easier to set up, use and maintain.
- You can make accessing your data more secure by adding what is known as Secured Socket Layer technology.

There are three components we need to work with when we use RDS. The first one, which is similar to TDC, resides on the client-side. It provides both data binding for the web page elements and a way of communicating with the middle-tier web server. The second component is the middle programme (object) which does the actual reading and writing to the specified ODBC data source. The third component is our actual database which has to be on ODBC-compliant database. The use of data binding requires a good understanding of object-oriented programming and how ODBC works, and the ability to use JavaScript.

Downloadable fonts

If you have more than one browser installed on your machine or even the same browser with two different settings, you will find the view of a web page may differ between the two browsers or two different settings. Covering this can be annoying especially after you have worked hard on your DHTML web pages only to find out that they are not viewed in the way you wanted. Downloadable fonts come to the rescue in this case. This is a technique that allows you to enhance your web page with your choice of fonts which will then be downloaded with the web page. It may all seem simple but does require careful thought.

First you have to have a font. To do so you have to either create the font, buy it or download from the Internet. It may help if you search using the font, font buy or font free keywords. Fonts are usually copyrighted so when you use a font as a downloadable font, make sure you have the right to do so. Once you install the font or fonts you want to use on your system – you must do this before using them – you have to create what is called a font definition file. To do this there are tools such as Font Composer Plug-in for Netscape Communicator. Then you can link the font definition file into your web documents using either the **STYLE** or **LINK** tags. Once you have done so you can use the font through the **FONT** or **STYLE** tags. The first time you use a downloadable font there is a lot of work involved, but it is very easy to repeat the procedure.

What is next?

When you have mastered the basics of DHTML that are presented in this book you will be able to use them creatively to build more lively web pages. There is no limit to what you can do with DHTML if you understand DHTML basics, in particular:

- Cascading Style Sheets (CSS).
- Layers.
- Document Object Model (DOM).
- Dynamic positioning.
- Dynamic contents.
- Data binding.
- Downloadable fonts.
- Scripting.

While there is very little to add to what we have covered in this book about these topics, we have only introduced scripting briefly. There is much more to learn, especially when it is combined with DOM. Finding a good source that defines the objects within DOM and their methods, attributes and events, which may be used with these objects, will help in widening what you can do using scripting and DOM.

Looking at other sites will help to inspire you with new ideas. By viewing the sites' sources you can see which techniques they have used. As DHTML is still evolving it is sensible to keep an eye on new development. You can get more information through W3C web site on the development of DHTML and through Netscape and Microsoft web sites, especially about what has been already implemented in their browsers. Netscape and Microsoft web sites also include detailed information about Netscape and IE DOM. I have included the Internet addresses (URL) of these organisations and others in appendix A.

Appendix A:
Interesting Web Sites
To Explore

Introduction

This appendix includes some useful web addresses. Some of these are interesting interactive sites while others contain materials related to DHTML. When viewing these pages try to examine the different aspects of interactive and dynamic techniques used. Some of these pages misuse multimedia effects while others manage to use them effectively to create very attractive sites.

Business and finance

American Express
    http://www.americanexpress.com/
Business Week
    http://www.businessweek.com/
CNNfn – markets
    http://www.cnnfn.com/markets/
Dow Jones
    http://bis.dowjones.com/
Economist
    http://www.economist.com/
Financial Times
    http://www.ft.com/
Harvard Business Press
    http://www.hbsp.harvard.edu/

Computer general

HTML
A Beginner's Guide to HTML
  http://www.ncsa.uiuc.edu/General/Internet/WWW/HTMLPrimer.html
HTML Quick Reference
  http://www.ncsa.uiuc.edu/General/Internet/WWW/HTMLQuickRef.html
  http://www.ucc.ie/~pflynn/books/htmlcard.html
Web Servers Directory
  http://www.w3.org/hypertext/DataSources/WWW/Servers.html

Web reference
Welcome to the Matrix
  http://www.reach.com/matrix/
Webmaster Reference Library
  http://ic.corpnet.com:80/~aking/webinfo/
Authors & Webmasters Forum
  http://mirror.wwa.com/mirror/msgs/html.htm
A CGI Programmer's Reference
  http://www.best.com/~hedlund/cgi-faq/
Spike's Place
  http://www.spikesplace.net/
The Groove Box
  http://www.groove-box.com/
Classifieds2000
  http://www.classifieds2000.com/
E-cards
  http://www.e-cards.com/
Blue Mountain
  http://www.bluemountain.com/
Angelfire
  http://angelfire.lycos.com/
Star Wars web site
  http://www.starwars.com/
Cool-LinkZ
  http://www.cool-linkz.com/
Yellow Pages
  http://www.yellowpages.com/
Hemmington Scott web site
  http://www.hemscott.com/
Hotmail
  http://www.hotmail.com/

Tools
WWW Software products and tools
    http://www.w3.org/hypertext/WWW/Status.html
    http://www.w3.org/hypertext/WWW/Tools/Overview.html
    http://www.hemac.com

Java and JavaScript
Netscape's JavaScript Authoring Guide
    http://www.netscape.com/eng/mozilla/Gold/handbook/javascript/index.html
    http://www.netscape.com/comprod/products/navigator/version_2.0/script/index.html
Sun Java Applet Index
    http://java.sun.com/applets/applets/index.html
Netscape's Java Applets
    http://www.netscape.com/comprod/products/navigator/version_2.0/java_applets/inde
x.html

Browsers and Internet software companies
Opera Software
    http://www.operasoftware.com
Netscape
    http://www.netscape.com/
Microsoft
    http://www.microsoft.com/

Search engines and free email addresses
LookSmart
    http://www.looksmart.com/
WebCrawler
    http://webcrawler.com/
Search Engine Directory
    http://www.dnc.net/users/king/search.htm
Yahoo
    www.yahoo.com/
Email address lookup
    http://www.iaf.net/
Excite
    http://www.excite.com/

Lifestyle

Virtual Flowers Homepage
    http://www.virtualflowers.com/
Virtual Vineyards
    http://www.virtualvin.com/
Shopping.com
    http://www.shopping.com/

Internet Card Central
   http://www.cardcentral.net/
Gardening and Landscaping
   http://www.btw.com/garden.htm
   http://www.garden.com/
Amazon.com - Virtual Bookstore
   http://www.amazon.com/
Books.com (US)
   http://www.books.com/
TitleFinder (UK)
   http://www.titlefinder.com/
Virtual Tourist
   http://www.vtourist.com/
Wines on the Internet
   http://www.wines.com/wines.html
City.Net
   http://www.city.net/

International news

CNN Interactive (US)
   http://www.cnn.com/
BBC News (UK)
   http://news.bbc.co.uk/text_only.htm
E-News
   http://www.enews.com/
Le Monde (FR)
   http://www.lemonde.fr/
De Telegraaf (NL)
   http://www.telegraaf.nl/
Die Zeit (D)
   http://www.zeit.de/
Der Standard (Austria)
   http://derstandard.at/Textversion/TOSeite1.htm
Financial Mail (ZA)
   http://www.fm.co.za/
Newspapers on the Web
   http://www.webwombat.com.au/intercom/newsprs/
USA Today (US)
   http://www.usatoday.com/

Humour

Laughing Internet (Main)

http://www.kilo.net/tli/index.html
Oracle Humor
   http://www.oraclehumor.com/
United Media Comics
   http://www.unitedmedia.com/
Humor archive
   http://www.cybercheeze.com/
Comedy Central Online
   http://www.comcentral.com/
Daily Humor
   http://www.daily-humor.com/jotd.html
the ONION | America's Finest News Source
   http://www.theonion.com/

Appendix B: HTML Tags

Introduction

Here is a selection of HTML tags divided into two main groups. Basic HTML tags are the standard HTML tags and work almost on all World Wide Web (WWW) browsers. The second group is the new tags that are used in DHTML. These tags work on most browsers but they may give different effects from one browser to another. Tags in both groups often take attributes. The tags are organised by appearance in the book and some attributes have been mentioned.

Basic HTML tags

Tags	Attributes
<HTML> ... </HTML>	
<BODY> ... </BODY>	
<HEAD> ... </HEAD>	
<TITLE> ... </TITLE>	
<H1> ... </H1>	
<H2> ... </H2>	
<H3> ... </H3>	
<FONT> ... </FONT>	
<OL> ... </OL>	
<UL> ... </UL>	
<LI> ... </LI>	
<TABLE> ... </TABLE>	
<TD> ... </TD>	
<TR> ... </TR>	

<A> ... </A>	HREF, TARGET
<FORM> ... </FORM>	METHOD, ACTION
<SELECT> ... </SELECT>	NAME
<OPTION> ... </OPTION>	NAME
<INPUT> ... </INPUT>	VALUE, TYPE, NAME
<FRAMESET> ... </FRAMESET>	COLS, ROWS
<FRAME> ... </FRAME>	
<NOFRAME> ... </NOFRAME>	
<IMG> ... </IMG>	NAME, SRC, DYNSRC, USEMAP
<BGSOUND> ... </BGSOUND>	NAME, SRC
<EMBED> ... </EMBED>	NAME, SRC
<APPLET> ... </APPLET>	

Basic DHTML tags

Tags	Attributes
<STYLE> ... </STYLE>	
<DIV> ... </DIV>	STYLE
<SPAN> ... </SPAN>	STYLE
<LAYER> ... </LAYER>	ID, WIDTH, TOP
<ILAYER> ... </ILAYER>	ID, WIDTH, TOP
<NOLAYER> ... </NOLAYER>	
<OBJECT> ... </OBJECT>	

 *Index*

The Essential Series

Editor: John Cowell

If you are looking for an accessible and quick introduction to a new language or area then these are the books for you.

Covering a wide range of topics including virtual reality, computer animation, Java, and Visual Basic to name but a few, the books provide a quick and accessible introduction to the subject. **Essentials** books let you start developing your own applications with the minimum of fuss - and fast.

The last few pages of this book are devoted to giving brief information about three of the other titles in this series.

All books are, of course, available from all good booksellers (who can order them even if they are not in stock), but if you have difficulties you can contact the publishers direct, by telephoning +44 1483 418822 (in the UK and Europe), +1/212/4 60 15 00 (in the USA), or by emailing orders@svl.co.uk

www.springer.co.uk   www.springer.de
www.springer-ny.com

Essential
Visual Basic 6.0 *fast*

John Cowell

Visual Basic is a mature and powerful, integrated development environment which allows you to create professional Windows applications. It has an intuitive user interface, an extensive set of components and excellent debugging facilities, so, whether you are a professional programmer or a student, this book tells you everything you need to know to write professional applications for Windows using Visual Basic 6.0.

Version 6.0 is the latest version of Visual Basic and includes all of the facilities of earlier versions combined with an extensive set of new controls. These greatly extend the capabilities for writing database and web-based applications.

Once you've read this book, you'll know all about:
- The Visual Basic language.
- The standard Visual Basic controls.
    - Handling control events.
    - Using data aware controls.
    - Creating and using ActiveX controls.
    - Writing web-based applications.

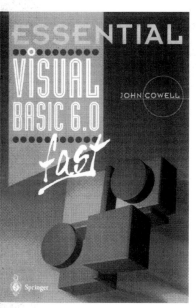

Essential Visual Basic 6.0 fast is designed for professional developers and students who need to learn the maximum in the minimum time and to develop applications *fast*.

224 pages
Softcover
ISBN 1-85233-207-7

Please see page 155 for ordering details

Essential
Visual C++ 6.0 *fast*

An Introduction to
Windows Programming
Using the Microsoft Foundation
Class Library

Ian Chivers

Microsoft's Visual C++ 6.0 contains lots of new features
designed to help developers build high performance
applications. This book is ideal reading if you want a
quick introduction to Windows programming using
Visual C++ and the Microsoft Foundation class (MFC)
library.

You'll find out all about...
- The 2 key Windows classes: CFrameWnd and
  CWinApp
- Message Maps
- Controls
- Graphical Output

And lots, lots more! *Essential Visual C++
6.0 fast* will help you create your own
applications - using all the exciting, new
features - quickly, effectively and
productively.

224 pages
Softcover
ISBN 1-85233-107-4

Please see page 155 for ordering details

Essential Computer Animation *fast*

How to Understand the Techniques and Potential of Computer Animation

John Vince

Computer Animation is now worlds away from its early beginnings when programs merely mimicked the hand drawn cartoon process. It's now regularly used for creating wonderful special effects in major movies like Titanic, Toy Story, Antz and A Bugs Life.

John Vince tells you all about:
- the basic principles used in the powerful software products currently available on the market
- the terms and processes involved
- and in an easy-to-understand way, with no complicated math.

Includes colour page section

So if you want to learn more about 3D computer animation without being swamped by complex mathematics, then read this book and have fun creating your own animated programs.

184 pages
Softcover
ISBN 1-85233-141-0

Please see page 155 for ordering details